CHARLES DEMUTH

CHARLES DEMUTH

by Alvord L. Eiseman

Watson-Guptill Publications/New York

Front cover: *On Stage*, 1915
Watercolor and pencil on paper, 11″ × 8¼″ (27.9 × 21 cm)
Private Collection

Paperback Edition, 1986

First published 1982 in the United States and Canada
by Watson-Guptill Publications, a division of Billboard Publications, Inc.
1515 Broadway, New York, N.Y. 10036

Library of Congress Catalog Card Number: 82-6930
ISBN 0-8230-1303-0

Distributed in the United Kingdom by Phaidon Press Ltd.,
Littlegate House, St. Ebbe's St., Oxford

Manufactured in Japan

1 2 3 4 5 6 7 8 9/91 90 89 88 87 86

LIST OF PLATES

Plate 1	SPRING CLOUDS	*Page* 32
Plate 2	COASTAL SCENE *or* ETRETAT	32
Plate 3	HOUSETOPS, SEASHORE	35
Plate 4	FLOWER PIECE	37
Plate 5	ALLOVER PATTERN OF LILACS	37
Plate 6	MARSHALL'S	39
Plate 7	IN VAUDEVILLE: THE GREEN DANCER	39
Plate 8	NANA, SEATED LEFT, AND SATIN AT LAURE'S RESTAURANT	40
Plate 9	TROPICAL PLANTS	42
Plate 10	LANDSCAPE	42
Plate 11	THE CIRCUS	44
Plate 12	EIGHT O'CLOCK—EVENING	46
Plate 13	DANCING SAILORS	46
Plate 14	ACROBATS	48
Plate 15	IN VAUDEVILLE: BIRD WOMAN	48
Plate 16	RED-ROOFED HOUSES	50
Plate 17	RED CHIMNEYS	50
Plate 18	IN VAUDEVILLE: DANCER WITH CHORUS	52
Plate 19	FLORA AND THE GOVERNESS	54
Plate 20	DELPHINIUM	57
Plate 21	FLOWERS	57
Plate 22	MARCHER RECEIVES HIS REVELATION AT MAY BARTRAM'S TOMB	59
Plate 23	BOX OF TRICKS	61
Plate 24	BUILDINGS	61
Plate 25	TIGER LILIES	63
Plate 26	RUE DU SINGE QUI PÊCHE	64
Plate 27	MODERN CONVENIENCES	65
Plate 28	FROM THE GARDEN OF THE CHÂTEAU	67
Plate 29	YELLOW CALLA LILY LEAVES	69
Plate 30	APPLES AND GREEN GLASS	68
Plate 31	BOWL OF ORANGES	70
Plate 32	EGGPLANT, CARROTS, AND TOMATOES	70
Plate 33	MY EGYPT	73
Plate 34	LOVE, LOVE, LOVE (HOMAGE TO GERTRUDE STEIN)	72
Plate 35	FRUIT AND FLOWER	74
Plate 36	I SAW THE FIGURE FIVE IN GOLD (HOMAGE TO WILLIAM CARLOS WILLIAMS)	76
Plate 37	ZINNIAS WITH SCARLET SAGE	78
Plate 38	RED AND YELLOW GLADIOLI	79
Plate 39	GREEN PEARS	80
Plate 40	MAN AND WOMAN, PROVINCETOWN	81

CHRONOLOGY

1883. Born November 8, in Lancaster, Pennsylvania, to Ferdinand and Augusta Buckius Demuth.

1887. Injures hip, probably caused by a fall from his father's arms, which renders him permanently lame.

1889. Family moves to 118 East King Street in Lancaster, to a house, along with the tobacco shop, which had belonged to the Demuth family since the 1700s.

1899. Enters Franklin and Marshall Academy for a "scientific" certificate. Paints *Spring Clouds*, a watercolor.

1900–01. Enters Drexel Institute of Art in Philadelphia.

1902–05. Continues his studies at the Drexel Institute. One drawing, *Anna Held*, still exists. Meets William Carlos Williams, Marianne Moore, and Ezra Pound in Philadelphia.

1904. First trip to Europe. Studies art at one of the Parisian academies.

1906–07. Enters the Pennsylvania Academy of the Fine Arts and studies with Thomas Anschutz, William Merritt Chase, Hugh Breckenridge, and Henry McCarter.

1907–08. Second trip to Europe. Visits Paris and Berlin. Several sketches from the Paris trip still exist.

1908–09. Continues his studies at the Pennsylvania Academy of Fine Arts. Vacations with Robert Locher on Monhegan Island, Maine.

1910. Spends his fifth and final year at the Pennsylvania Academy of Fine Arts. Completes many pen and watercolor sketches, as well as scenes of Lancaster and of his parents.

1911. Father dies. Charles stays at home with his mother settling the estate.

1912–14. First exhibition at the Pennsylvania Academy's annual watercolor show. Also exhibits at the Woolworth Building in Lancaster. Took his third and probably most important trip to Europe, where he attended the Academies Julian, Moderne, and Colarossi. Meets Gertrude and Leo Stein and Alice Toklas. Travels with Marsden Hartley to Berlin and meets Arnold Rönnebeck who sculpts the only bust of Demuth. Paints at Étretat. Begins work on the Henry James illustrations. Writes a one-act play, *The Azure Adder*, published in *The Glebe*.

1914. Summers in Provincetown, where he meets Eugene O'Neill and works with the Provincetown Players.

1914–15. First one-man show at the Charles Daniel Gallery in New York. Spends most of the year in Lancaster, with frequent visits to New York, where he stayed at the Hotel Brevoort. Begins the cafe and *In Vaudeville* genres.

1915–16. Keeps a studio on Washington Square in New York, but then moves back to Lancaster. Meets Marcel Duchamp, Francis Picabia, and Albert Gleizes. Second one-man show at the Daniel Gallery.

1916–17. Visits Bermuda, along with Marsden Hartley, Albert Gleizes, Louis Bouche, and is strongly influenced by Cubism. Begins the Bermuda landscape series and the window motif florals. Third one-man show at the

Daniel Gallery. Summers at Gloucester, where he continues to paint the cubist-styled landscapes. This is the most fruitful period of Demuth's career.

1917–18. Fourth show at the Daniel Gallery, which is shared with his friend Edward Fisk. Summers in Provincetown, where he incorporates the Bermuda style with the architectural landscapes of New England and Lancaster.

1918–19. Fifth show at the Daniel Gallery. Begins to show signs of chronic illness.

1919–21. Works on the temperas of Gloucester, Provincetown, and Lancaster, employing Duchampian titles and prismatic effects. Sixth show at the Daniel Gallery. Makes last trip to Europe where he is hospitalized at Neuilly-sur-Seine for one week. Convalesces at Dr. Allen's Sanatorium in Morristown, New Jersey. Works primarily in oil on the architectural and industrial landscapes.

1922–23. Seventh exhibition at the Daniel Gallery. Works mainly on the floral watercolors and begins the still lifes.

1924–25. Eighth and final show at the Daniel Gallery. First exhibit at Alfred Stieglitz's Intimate Gallery, which includes his poster portraits of Georgia O'Keeffe and Arthur Dove.

1926–27. First one-man show at the Intimate Gallery. Awarded a silver medal for the watercolor *Plums* at the Philadelphia Sesquicentennial Exposition. Also awarded the Dana Watercolor Medal for *Roses* at the Pennsylvania Academy's "24th Annual Watercolor Exhibition." Works mainly on watercolor still lifes, but also paints *My Egypt* and *Longhi on Broadway*.

1928–29. Second one-man show at the Intimate Gallery. Also represented at the "27th International Exhibition" of the Carnegie Institute in Pittsburgh and at The Museum of Modern Art. Paints *I Saw The Figure Five In Gold*.

1930. Returns to the industrial landscapes in oil and completes most of the so-called "pornographic" watercolors. Participates in a group exhibition at Alfred Stieglitz's An American Place Gallery and also in The Museum of Modern Art's Summer Exhibition: "Retrospective."

1931. One-man show at An American Place Gallery and also represented at Edith Gregor Halpert's "Seven Masters of Watercolor" at the Downtown Gallery.

1932. Represented in "Impromptu Exhibition of Selected Paintings" at An American Place Gallery, and was included in The Museum of Modern Art's "American Paintings and Sculpture 1862–1932."

1933. Exhibits at the Whitney Musuem of American Art's "First Biennial Exhibition of Contemporary American Painting."

1934. Included in the "19th International Biennial Art Exhibition," Venice, Italy, and in "Five Americans," an exhibit at the Smith College Museum of Art. Returns to Provincetown in the summer, where he produces his sketchbook of beach scenes.

1935. Becomes ill on the train on the way home from New York to Lancaster. Dies October 23 in his own bedroom.

SELF-PORTRAIT, *1907. Oil on canvas. 26 × 18 in. (66 × 45.7 cm). Private collection.*

Charles Demuth

Figure 1. The Demuth family's tobacco shop in Lancaster, Pennsylvania.

Figure 2. The young Charles with his mother and aunt in the garden of his home at 118 East King Street.

CHARLES Henry Buckius Demuth was born at 109 North-line Street in Lancaster, Pennsylvania, on November 8, 1883, the son of Ferdinand Andrew and Augusta Wills Buckius Demuth. Shortly before the family moved to 118 East King Street, next to their family-owned tobacco shop, Demuth's father accidentally dropped the boy while they were playing. The four-year-old sustained a serious injury to his hip that left him bedridden during his preschool years. For the rest of his life, as a result of this injury, Demuth had to wear an orthopedic shoe and he walked with a limp. It was during the time that he was bedridden that the young Demuth became interested in painting.

The Demuth family had rather strong artistic interests. Charles's father was a talented amateur photographer, two great-aunts were watercolorists, his grandfather was a sculptor, and the Pennsylvania artists Aaron Eshleman and Jacob Eichholtz were distant relatives. Both Demuth's mother and his aunt, Kate Buckius, encouraged the boy's artistic efforts, and thanks to his mother, some of his earliest sketches still exist. It is important to note that the family was financially comfortable for the times and therefore willingly financed Charles's art studies, as well as his career.

With the sole exception of his Parisian studies in 1912–14, Charles Demuth was educated near home—in Philadelphia, in the Lancaster public schools, at the nearby Franklin and Marshall Academies, and with private tutors. In 1901 he left home for the first time to enter the Drexel Institute in Philadelphia, where he remained until the spring of 1907, when the art department was dissolved. From 1905 until 1911 he also attended the Pennsylvania Academy of Fine Arts. In both schools the strong influence of Thomas Eakins was felt, and two of Charles's instructors, Thomas Anschutz and William Merritt Chase, had been pupils of Eakins. Even more significant, however, during these Drexel years was his meeting William Carlos Williams, Marianne Moore, Ezra Pound, and probably Man Ray, who were all in Philadelphia at this time. His friendships with the medico-poet Williams and with the photographer-painter Ray would continue for the whole of Demuth's life and greatly influence all three men.

The years at the Pennsylvania Academy of Fine Arts were undoubtedly some of the happiest for the artist. Under Anschutz, Hugh Breckenridge, and his favorite instructor, Henry McCarter, Demuth blossomed. He found himself admired not only by his fellow students but by most of his instructors as well. Even so, Demuth already showed signs of independence. He questioned the teachings of Hugh Breckenridge, calling them bombastic and derivative. He admired Henry McCarter, who had studied under the nineteenth-century French mural painter Pierre Puvis de Chavannes, and also the work of the Impressionists and their followers. It was at McCarter's urging that Demuth took his second trip to Paris in 1907–08, when he also visited Berlin. Unfortunately, little is known about this visit except that it caused a change in Demuth's work. One watercolor, a floral study titled *After Paris*, has the vivid colors and style of Fauvism, which was a major stylistic movement during Demuth's formative years.

Although Demuth made four trips to Europe, frequently visited New York and Philadelphia, and painted in various places around

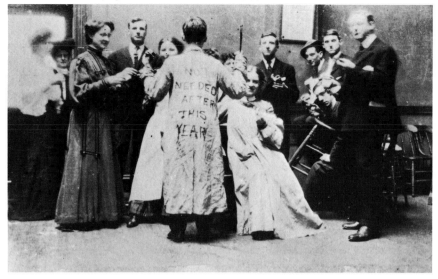

Pennsylvania and New Jersey, most of his work was either started or completed on East King Street in Lancaster in his bedroom-studio. After his second trip to Europe, he re-enrolled at the Pennsylvania Academy, where he remained until 1911, when his father died. He then returned to Lancaster for a year to help his mother settle his father's estate. At this time Demuth had not yet found his own artistic style and was still experimenting with the divergent styles of Chase and McCarter, of the Fauves, and even of his great-aunts.

T HE YEAR 1910 marked the beginning of another important and long-lasting influence on Demuth's life—his homosexual relationship with Robert Locher. The two had known each other since childhood because the Locher farm, "Old Top," adjoined the Buckius family farm, but not until 1910, on a trip to Monhegan Island, Maine, did they become more intimate. Although their homosexual relationship was kept discreet, it remained a constant throughout their lives. Charles began to encourage the younger Robert to begin his own art career, which he did. Years later Locher became a stage designer for Florenz Ziegfeld, as well as designing the interiors for the Eighth Street Whitney Museum of American Art.

Although Demuth was by no means wealthy, his inheritance from his father's estate allowed him to be financially independent for the rest of his life and gave him the freedom to devote himself fully to painting. By 1912 he had exhibited in the Pennsylvania Academy's annual watercolor show, and at the new Woolworth Building in Lancaster. In December of that same year family matters were

sufficiently settled so that Demuth could make his next, and possibly most important, trip to Paris and Étretat, where he remained until the spring of 1914. While in Paris he joined the Academie Moderne and also worked at the Academies Colarossi and Julien. For the first time he traveled to Étretat, in Normandy, and possibly even to Cornwall, England. Many of his famous seascape paintings are of this fishing village on the coast of France. *Coastal Scene* or *Étretat* (Plate 2) is one of the finest examples of these watercolors, which also show that Demuth not only was experimenting toward ever greater purity of style but was moving steadily ahead in perfecting his control of the medium. In *House-tops, Seashore* (Plate 3) he exhibits an astounding ability reminiscent of Paul Klee's watercolors.

It was also during this visit to France that Demuth met Leo and Gertrude Stein, Sherwood Anderson, and Alice Toklas, and was introduced through Alfred Stieglitz to Marsden Hartley and Edward Fisk. He revisited Berlin with Hartley and became friends with Arnold Rönnebeck. During his two visits to Berlin, he probably saw the works of the Die Brücke and Der Blaue Reiter groups, the German Expressionists, and the paintings of Kandinsky and Klee. His graceful figure drawings of this period reflect his familiarity with the works of Rodin; he also assimilated the colors of the Fauves in his early watercolors and oils, having seen the paintings by Picasso, Matisse, Gris, and others in the superb collection of the Steins.

By the time Demuth returned from Europe, he had realized that his favorite medium was to be watercolor. His mastery of it can be seen in such works as *Allover Pattern of Lilacs*

Figure 4. ON STAGE, *1915.*
Watercolor and pencil on paper.
11 × 8¼ in. (27.9 × 21 cm).
Private collection.

(Plate 5) and *On Stage* (Figure 4), an early example in his *In Vaudeville* series. As these watercolors illustrate, Demuth used the entire page when he painted, covering it completely. Such works as *Flower Piece* (Plate 4) are very typical of his floral studies of this period. They not only fill the page but are wonderfully explosive and appear to move toward the sun.

Soon after Demuth's return from Europe in 1914, he had his first one-man show at the Daniel Gallery in New York, which was followed by a second one in 1915. He maintained a small studio on Washington Square for a while, but most of his stays in New York were at the Hotel Brevoort, then located at Eighth Street and Fifth Avenue. Demuth could be seen limping along the Greenwich Village streets, meeting his friends at Romany Marie's, The Golden Swan, Polly Holliday's, and many other such places. Not only could he indulge his sexual inclinations at the nearby Lafayette Baths or the still closer ones at St. Mark's Place, but the Village was the meeting ground for the Provincetown Players and other artists' groups.

By this time Demuth was also being welcomed into most of the "salons" of New York and Philadelphia. These were the years of the Arensbergs, Mabel Dodge Luhan, and the Stettheimer group, which included Virgil Thomson, Gertrude Stein in exile, Carl Van Vechten and his wife, Fania Marinoff, and the art critic Henry McBride. Among Demuth's friends in New York were Eugene and Agnes O'Neill, Susan Glaspell, George Cram Cook, and later Stuart Davis. In Philadelphia there were the Bories, the S.S. Whites III, Jules Pascin, and the Biddles. The places and people with whom Demuth associated, enjoying a

life very different from that of Lancaster, are depicted in such works as the several versions of the black nightclub Marshall's and in various cafe scenes.

DEMUTH began to spend his summers in Provincetown, Massachusetts, which would become his summer home for almost the remainder of his life. In fact, most of his beach scenes and seascapes were painted there. The early years in Provincetown are best described in a letter written by the artist Stuart Davis, who stated: "On clear days the air and the water had a brilliance of light greater than I had ever seen. While this tended to destroy local color, it stimulated the desire to invent high intensity color intervals. . . . The presence of artists and writers, not too many, added intellectual stimulus to the natural charm of the place. I met Charles Demuth, and his superior knowledge of what it was all about was a great help to me."[1]

It was in Provincetown that Demuth became friends with Eugene O'Neill, at the writer's Coast Guard Station home. Demuth enjoyed sharing a drink, and this was, of course, the reputation of the young O'Neill. But the artist enjoyed even more the company of O'Neill's wife, Agnes Boulton O'Neill, and their baby, Shane. He also enjoyed hearing O'Neill's stories of his sea voyages, of his emerging plays, and the stories of his father, the actor James O'Neill. But beyond the drinking and the shared tales, Demuth and O'Neill clearly respected each other's talents, and they even worked together on several Provincetown Players projects. They also met

Figure 5. FEMALE NUDE FIGURE #6,
c. 1912–14. Watercolor and pencil on paper.
Courtesy Santa Fe East, Santa Fe, New Mexic

during the wintertime in Greenwich Village. Both were friends of the Hollidays, Polly and Louis, and together they frequented such places as The Golden Swan (the "Hell-Hole," which later became the locale for O'Neill's *The Iceman Cometh*).

In spite of, but perhaps because of, O'Neill's difficult personality, an intense friendship developed between these two very different men. In O'Neill's play *Strange Interlude*, which is concerned with the subconscious as consciously stated, the leading male character is called Charlie Marsden, who is clearly a composite of Demuth and Marsden Hartley. Demuth reciprocated by painting the Poster Portrait *Longhi on Broadway* (Figure 14), which is his compliment to Eugene O'Neill.

B Y EARLY 1915 Demuth had started work on the illustrations for Émile Zola's *Nana* and his famed watercolor series. That year was important to his creative development in another way. Marcel Duchamp arrived from France and was introduced to Demuth by the Arensbergs and Carl Van Vechten. Duchamp and Demuth became fast friends and formed a mutual admiration society that lasted even after Demuth's death.

The years of 1915 and most of 1916–17 produced at least a quarter of Demuth's total oeuvre. The artist set for himself a new concept of inherent purity, of less being more, and developed a new and thoroughly consistent artistic sensibility. He has been quoted as saying he was under the direct influence of Duchamp, whom he thought of as "stranger than any of us—and that's writing a lot! But a great painter. The big glass thing, I think, is still the great picture of our time."[2]

In 1916 Demuth joined Marsden Hartley on the British island of Bermuda, which was in the midst of the war. Albert Gleizes, the Cubist painter and author, and Louis Bouché, another painter, were in Bermuda at this time too. These four artists must surely have gotten together on this small island and had long discussions on the new Cubism, the German Expressionists, the Italian Futurists, Dada, and Surrealism.

That year two very distinct changes appeared in Demuth's style. The first change was seen in his flower paintings, which he did in oil and tempera. They were very different from anything else that he had ever painted and very close in style to the kind of work done by Hartley. Demuth's *Cottage Window* is a superb example of this heavy, impasto style. In most of his paintings from this period the window frame and sill are shown, to serve as a decorative definition of the space utilized. At no other time did Demuth apply paint so thickly.

Even more radical, however, was the change in the watercolors he painted while in Bermuda. During this time, Demuth was able to digest the many new elements in the artistic styles he had seen in France, Germany, and New York. Not only did he admire the abstractionist and Cubist styles of Duchamp, Matisse, Picasso, O'Keeffe, Hartley, and Dove, but he was able to assimilate them into his own strong, individualistic style. The sinuous flowers erupting from the soil, the Fauvish-colored seascapes and mountains, and even the song-and-dance themes slowly began to give way to cubes and prisms. Serpentine

tree trunks, branches, and leaves began to contrast with the block forms of houses. Even Demuth's still lifes of a later period maintain the contrast of pristine fruit and flowers against flowing drapes and cloths.

Beginning with his Bermuda works, such as *Landscape* (Plate 10), 1916, Demuth covered the paper or the canvas less and less and gave the background importance equal to the subject painted. His new style, later called "Precisionism," was merely his own method of combining what he found effective in the many new painterly elements and making them his own.

The year 1916 appears to have been his most creative year, not only in the number of works he produced, but in the changes that occurred while he was in Bermuda. The *Nana* illustrations, oils such as *Cottage Window*, a plethora of drawings, a good part of his "trees" series, watercolor florals, many *In Vaudeville* paintings, part of the Bermuda landscapes, and other works mark it as his most prolific and versatile period.

By 1917 Demuth had reached an aesthetic maturity that he continued to refine and recreate in ever new variations and nuances. His paintings of this period reach a new height in sensitivity of design, media control, composition, delicacy, color, and intensity that is difficult to parallel. The many "tree" studies of 1916–17 have a conciseness of rhythm and unity that can be found in early Chinese paintings or in similar works by Cézanne. In these formative years of 1916 to 1918, the diversity of genre that Demuth worked in and the works that he created are quite astounding—from cafe scenes to pictures of circus life to more personal paintings of dancing sailors and scenes of nightlife.

ALL OF his works, starting with 1916, began to utilize the blotter method of watercolor, in which watercolor is carefully applied with a brush, then wiped away before drying. This technique created both textural effects and the evanescent qualities that became an essential part of Demuth's work. Such works as *Dancing Sailors* (Plate 13), his series about the Hotel Brevoort, entitled the *"Eight O'Clocks,"* and his later illustrations for the tales of Henry James characterize Demuth's expertise in watercolor and his splendid capabilities using the blotter method.

By 1918 all of Demuth's paintings and illustrations show his mastery of technique, his knowledge of where and how to distort, and his never failing sense of composition. It is interesting to note that most of the acrobatic, vaudeville, and circus scenes were drawn *in situ* at the two theaters in Lancaster—the Fulton Opera House and the Colonial. Repertory theater, as well as many fine vaudeville acts, tried out in small-town theaters such as the two in Lancaster. Among the greats Demuth saw and recorded on the Fulton stage were the Barrymores, George M. Cohan, Minnie Maddern Fiske, Sarah Bernhardt, W. C. Fields, and Al Jolson. Demuth not only enjoyed the performances but, as reflected in his paintings, had the same empathy for acrobats and song-and-dance teams that Toulouse-Lautrec had for dance-hall girls, and Degas his ballet gamines. A sense of the trials and effort that went on before and during each act and the desire of each performer to please the audience are important elements in the *In Vaudeville* series. Like Lautrec and Degas, Demuth, possibly because of his lameness,

painted the exertions of the performers as if they were his own.

In his illustrations for *The Turn of the Screw* and *The Beast in the Jungle,* two of Henry James's tales that are often described as his masterpieces, Demuth, just as in his theater and circus scenes, deeply empathized with the characters and chose the decor and color with unfaltering taste. In these works, which were painted simultaneously with the Bermuda landscapes, trees, and houses, the labels of Precisionism and Cubist-Realism become highly inappropriate. Demuth's illustrations for James's tales, as well as those for Zola's *Nana* and *L'Assomoir,* Franz Wedekind's *Die Büchse der Pandora* and *Erdgeist,* and Edgar Allan Poe's *The Masque of the Red Death,* are each in their own way very sensitive to the mood of the story. The variation within each of these illustrations is remarkable. The mystical, emotional quality, particularly for the ghost stories of Henry James, is as perceptive and subtly conceived as the stories themselves.

By 1918 the painter's creative growth was constant. The amount of work Demuth did in this year would never again be equaled. He put the lessons of refinement and Cubistic purity that were learned in Bermuda to unique use in such works as *Red Chimneys* or in the fantastic flowers that once again started to emerge from his brush. The landscapes he did at this time demonstrate his ease in technique and a relish in his sense of the mysterious within the everyday environs of Provincetown, Gloucester, and Lancaster. Demuth's sense of structure and composition had reached an acme, which only the artist himself could better.

By 1919, although he had had his fifth showing at the Daniel Gallery, Demuth was becoming very dissatisfied with Charles Daniel, even tearing his own work in fours when he felt it had been insufficiently appreciated. At the same time he was becoming more and more an aficionado of Alfred Stieglitz. But even here Demuth maintained his individuality. He enjoyed talking and writing to Stieglitz, but it was mainly his sense of being with his fellow artists and compeers that made Demuth feel part of the Stieglitz group. He most enjoyed meeting and talking with Georgia O'Keeffe, then with John Marin and Arthur Dove, for each of whom he would eventually paint "homages." In his studio-bedroom hung O'Keeffe's *Two Avocados,* Marin's *Sunset,* and a Man Ray. During this time a chronic, but undiagnosed, illness became noticeable to his friends and relatives. It had the effect, as he explained in a letter to Stieglitz, of making watercolor painting, with its immediacy, and the equally demanding figure work frequently "too much" for him after 1919. The number of paintings Demuth painted that year diminished tremendously.

After 1919 Demuth turned to tempera and began painting his architectural landscapes. In these paintings Demuth reduced the forms to facets of light and used intersecting diagonals to suggest shafts of light and shadow. Although *In the Province,* which was painted in 1919, is spare and simple, it also reveals the beginnings of the fragmenting of the sky areas and the closing-in of the open spaces imposed on the architecture of Lancaster. As Demuth continued to paint these temperas, they slowly became more complex. In *After Sir Christopher Wren* (or *New England*) the sky's ocher and sand colors are patterned like an Amish

quilt and the buildings and church steeples are faceted like prisms.

Within the span of the next two years, 1919–1920, Demuth's work shows both the derivation of his Pennsylvania-Dutch heritage and the influence of Marcel Duchamp. *Stairs, Provincetown*, which depicts a back staircase in New England, refers to Duchamp's famed *Nude Descending a Staircase*. In his choice of titles Demuth shared a delight with his friend Duchamp. (Demuth's native wit has been testified to by his own family and his Lancaster friends.) At this time his feeling toward his hometown and Provincetown began to change. Although he spent his summers in Provincetown and painted most of his work in his studio on East King Street, his ambivalence toward the provincial attitudes of Lancaster became a dominant factor in his life.

DEMUTH'S feelings about the encroaching machine age were quite different than that of Picabia, Léger, the Synchronists, and the Italian Futurists' love of machinery, speed, and force. His *End of the Parade—Coatesville, Pa.* indicates by its subtle irony what he thought of these mills just a few miles away from Lancaster. In contrast the delicate, lightly painted landforms of *Dunes, Provincetown*, 1920, conveys the artist's more positive feeling for nature. This watercolor is quite the opposite of the vertical and prismatic architectural landscapes.

Demuth's other works completed in 1920 were all watercolors of flowers. In them he used the strong sense of color and form that he had learned in Bermuda and from the 1919–20 architectural works. But in these florals Demuth also applied his love of and familiarity with nature, so that there is a harmonious blending of influences.

The year 1921 was in every way a most crucial year for Charles Demuth. Despite several severe attacks of his still undiagnosed disease, and against the protests of family and friends, he embarked in midsummer to London and Paris. He met Marsden Hartley in the "City of Light," tried desperately to work, but became even more ill. There are several letters and postcards to his mother and to Alfred Stieglitz that describe his ill health, but they also indicate his strong wish not to come home. He felt that Paris and Europe were still "it," recounting to his family and friends Marcel Duchamp's fame. He sold two works to Leonce Rosenberg, a Parisian gallery, but even with this success, Demuth became so ill that he was hospitalized at the American Hospital, Neuilly-sur-Seine. Later, Hartley's lovely epitaph, "Farewell, Charles," would commemorate Demuth's realization that he was really very ill.

"O well, I've seen it all—I've done it all."
. . . Charles learns that he is really ill, and that he must go home. Summer was on the way of being over.[3]

However, Demuth's creative impulse had not, even then, diminished. While in Paris he managed to paint the exquisite *Rue du Singe Qui Pêche* (Plate 26), which is one of the few works he painted *in situ*. This painting also signaled a new stylistic approach. He began to incorporate signs and lettering into his work, which predates Stuart Davis's use of signs and would later influence the work of Pop artists such as Robert Indiana and Jasper Johns. During this period the colors of Demuth's palette became more somber, possibly reflecting his

Figure 10. Two photographs
made by Alfred Stieglitz
of the ill Demuth when he was
en route to the Morristown
sanitorium, Spring 1922.

failing health. But even while aboard the ship returning home, Demuth continued to paint, and for the first time, the terms Precisionist and Cubist-Realist became descriptive of the artist's painting style.

When he returned to Lancaster, Demuth's illness was diagnosed as diabetes. He was hospitalized at Dr. Allen's sanatorium for diabetics in Morristown, New Jersey, where he finished, during 1921, the following works: *Aucassin and Nicolette, Flour Mill* or *Factory, Lancaster, Business, Spring* (Figure 16), *Incense of a New Church, Nospmas M. Egiap Nospmas M., Architecture, Paquebot Paris* and *Welcome to Our City*.

These titles reflect the artist's ironic attitude toward the approaching machine age. *Spring* depicts a sampling of fabric swatches; *Business* is simply factory windows; *Incense of a New Church* shows the belching fumes of smokestacks; and *Aucassin and Nicolette*, the famed French lovers, are depicted as a smokestack and a water tower nestling against each other. All of these paintings, and particularly *Nospmas M. Egiap Nospmas M.*, which read backward becomes, enigmatically, "Sampson M. Paige Sampson M.," are Duchampian and reveal Demuth's caustic look at what was happening to the world, especially to his beloved Lancaster.

AFTER the onset of his illness, Demuth went from his normal slim frame to a shadow of his former self. It is remarkable that in the years that followed he was able to paint at all, but the creative impulse did not falter until the last years of his life. The only genre that he gave up during these years of illness was that of figure draw-

ing. It was not until 1930 that he did a few of the so-called "pornographic" watercolors and not until the last year of his life that he re-embarked on the beach scenes.

In 1922 Demuth returned to the watercolor medium and began painting the bulk of his still lifes. Flowers and vegetables became his themes. Perhaps because of his serious illness or his intense knowledge of how close to death he had come, the still lifes and the flower paintings of these years were painted with a rare tenderness. Such works as *Yellow Calla Lily Leaves* (Plate 29) and *Flower Study: White Tulips* not only exhibit this quality but also show the perfection of composition that is so representative of Demuth's work. They exemplify his use of "empty" space as an integral part of the whole painting. The floral watercolors of 1922 and 1923 all contain a characteristic diamond of triangular shape, often with foliage completing the diamond but never covering the entire page.

In 1923 Demuth had his eighth and final exhibition at the Daniel Gallery in New York. After that year he exhibited at Alfred Stieglitz's Gallery 291, where he remained until 1929, when he moved to the Kraushaar Gallery. The rapport between Demuth and Stieglitz was great. Demuth's admiration for Stieglitz came through not only in their dealer-artist relationship but also in Demuth's special reverence for the man who was the first to show Rodin drawings, Cézanne watercolors, children's art as art, and African art in the United States. Stieglitz's devotion to the artists he exhibited was as deep as his loathing for the average gallery-goer, critic, or collector. In one of his exhibition catalogues Stieglitz wrote, "All but time-killers are welcome."

By 1924 Demuth was happily ensconced in the Stieglitz circle. He was creating not only his still lifes but a whole new concept—his homages, or symbolic poster portraits. All of these portraits were tributes to the chosen few that Charles Demuth admired and thought of great importance. In 1924 he painted, all in oil on academy board, three finished poster portraits: *Arthur G. Dove, Georgia O'Keeffe*, and *Love, Love, Love (Homage to Gertrude Stein)*, as well as a watercolor study for Marsden Hartley and a study for the Dove portrait. *Love, Love, Love* (Plate 34) clearly demonstrates the symbolic imagery that is used in all of these homages. The reiteration of the word "Love," fully written only once, and the "1 2 3" imitates in paint Gertrude Stein's love of repetition. The painting is divided in half by a white mask, which seems to be a direct reference to Picasso's 1906 portrait of *Gertrude Stein*. The symbolism in all of the poster portraits is usually very clear and understandable, and in none of them does Demuth forget what he had learned from Duchamp and the spirit of Dada.

Even while Demuth was developing the innovative concept of the poster portrait, he was also painting some of his finest florals. The still lifes and florals of this period employ a unique combination of flowers and fruit. In these and in his poster portraits Demuth's use of space and his sensitivity to composition remain constant. Although the homages tend toward what would later be called Precisionism, they hardly hold to the stylistic elements of this genre. In these paintings Demuth defies absolute straight lines; he fades the letters, moves the geometric figures, books, and plants, and plays with them almost as in a Duchampian chess game. In 1925 these works were included in the Anderson Gallery's exhibition "Seven Americans—159 Paintings, Photographs and Things, Recent and Never Before Publically Shown." The exhibition included the work of Charles Demuth, Arthur Dove, Marsden Hartley, John Marin, Paul Strand, Georgia O'Keeffe, and Stieglitz—a very rarified group.

DEMUTH continued to use his flower and fruit motif, but by 1925 he introduced curvilinear forms into his still lifes. Such works as *Apples and Green Glass* (Plate 30), *Apples and Bananas*, and especially *Bowl of Oranges* (Plate 31) demonstrate this combination of curves and prismatic effects. Often the artist would devise a cloth, napkin, or drape to enfold the fruit and flowers or bowls and tableware.

In *Bowl of Oranges* (Plate 31) the intense color contrast of the blue rococo background with the brilliant oranges achieves and emulates the painting style that Demuth ascribed to Georgia O'Keeffe in his preface to one of her exhibitions.

> Flowers and flames. And color. Color as color, not as volume, or light—only as color. The last mad throb of red just as it turns green, the ultimate shriek of orange calling upon all the blues of heaven for relief or support; these Georgia O'Keeffe is able to use. In her canvases each color almost regains the fun it must have felt within itself, on forming the first rainbow.[4]

Demuth admired O'Keeffe. At one time he had even hoped to work on a flower painting

with her. And, of course, Demuth's words apply equally well to himself, from his early Fauvist oils and watercolors to the more opulent 1925 still lifes.

The flower watercolors of 1925 also show Demuth's use of the shell-like curve, and all of these florals exhibit the identical diamond shape. Demuth's technical proficiency in watercolor continued to increase. His use of the white of the paper to form flowers, leaves, foliage, and cloth became masterful.

The artist, with very little encouragement from anyone (he comments to Stieglitz that they are the only ones to like these works), continued to create his poster portraits, including two very great ones: *Charles Duncan* and *John Marin.* From 1921 on, Demuth's battle with diabetes never ceased, continuing to drain his energies. His output was now limited to one painting per week or even less. His reputation, however, was starting to increase. He won a silver medal at the Philadelphia Sesquicentennial Exposition and was awarded the Dana Watercolor medal at the Pennsylvania Academy of Fine Arts' Twenty-fourth Annual Philadelphia Watercolor Exhibition. He also had his second showing with Stieglitz, a one-man show at the Intimate Gallery in New York.

The year 1926 confirmed not only Demuth's spreading fame but also his disability, because in that year there were more "unfinished" works than in any other. Nevertheless, the work he did complete showed his striving for more simplicity and his ability to structure an almost completely curvilinear watercolor. He also began to paint a variety of still life subjects, such as *Grapes and Turnips; Carrots and Apples; Cheese, Fruit, and Vegetables; Oranges and Artichokes; Apples and Pears.*

All of the 1926 still lifes show far less emphasis on drapery and tablecloths than before; and beginning with these fruit and vegetable still lifes, the subjects themselves form the background that supports them. It is in these florals that Demuth's strange lack of completion is most evident—an effect most probably caused by the energy-draining diabetes.

By 1927, however, Demuth's inertia abated somewhat. In this year he painted *My Egypt* (Plate 33), which is considered to be one of his most important works. He also did another poster portrait entitled *Calla Lilies (Homage to Bert Savoy)* and a series of still lifes, all using the eggplant as subject matter. *Eggplant, Carrots, and Tomatoes* (Plate 32) is one of the finest of these studies.

My Egypt remains his 1927 masterpiece; it is here that the misnomers of Precisionism and Cubist-Realism start gathering like clouds around Demuth's image as a painter. The work itself is an ecological and social comment on the silos of the Eshleman Company of Lancaster. Demuth's native wit was released by Marcel Duchamp, and the titles of his works are often puns and anagrams, homonyms, and fun. The grain silos in *My Egypt* are meant to be the pyramids of Lancaster, Pennsylvania.

THE FACT that *My Egypt* is rather small (35¾ × 30 inches) is important; for as in most of Demuth's work, the sense of proportion, composition, and design makes the painting seem larger than it actually is. Demuth chose only what he wanted from reality. There is nothing extraneous in *My Egypt,* which is true of most of his work. Demuth used the sunlike rays, which have the quality of klieg lights at a movie pre-

miere, to give the oil its depth and magnitude. The balance of lights and darks in *My Egypt* is masterful, and the whites and off-whites of the two silos move upward almost magically. Everything within the painting serves its own particular stylistic and aesthetic purpose.

The year 1928 was equally important in Demuth's creative development because this was the year that included two of his finest poster portraits: *I Saw the Figure 5 in Gold* (*Homage to William Carlos Williams*) (Plate 36) and *Longhi on Broadway* (*Homage to Eugene O'Neill*) (Figure 13).

Charles Demuth's friendship with William Carlos Williams began in 1905 in Philadelphia when the two met at Mrs. Chain's boarding-house, supposedly over a dish of prunes, during Demuth's art school days at Drexel. Until Demuth's death in 1935, the two men would remain close friends, and Williams would come to write one of his most ambitious elegies for the artist. Although Demuth and Williams both contributed to *The Dial* and other avant-garde publications, they moved in very different circles. The poet was not only a well-known doctor in his native town of Rutherford, New Jersey, he was also a prolific writer and a husband and father. However, their deep regard for each other remained constant, and *I Saw the Figure 5 in Gold* was inspired by Williams's poem "The Great Figure."

Among the rain
and lights
I saw the figure 5
in gold
on a red
firetruck

moving
tense
unheeded
to gong clangs
siren howls
and wheels rumbling
through the dark city.[5]

DEMUTH's homage to his friendship with Eugene O'Neill first came in the form of a study for a poster portrait. Demuth then wrote to O'Neill's wife, Agnes, about it. She evidently spoke to her husband, who refused to have his name as prominently displayed as it was in the study. Demuth persevered, however, and *Longhi on Broadway* (*Homage to Eugene O'Neill*) emerged in 1928.

The enormous differences between *Longhi on Broadway* and *I Saw the Figure 5 in Gold* are almost as immeasurable as the personalities of the two subjects. The onrushing effect of the homage to Williams is typical not only of Williams's poetry but also his personality, while the symbolism of the homage to Eugene O'Neill is quite the opposite. The innate delicacy of O'Neill is reflected in this poster portrait as are the symbols of drama, the literary life, and even those that refer to O'Neill's drinking. The comparison of the two eighteenth-century father and son artists, the Longhis, with the actor-dramatist roles of the O'Neills was both apt and Duchampian.

Demuth painted one tempera during 1928, *Still Life with Spoon*, which is more similar to the poster portraits than to a still life. His florals of this year must rank with some of the

finest he ever did. Among them are *Zinnias with Scarlet Sage* (Plate 37) and the equally exquisite *Bouquet of Jonquils.* There are at least nine of these flower watercolors, which are characterized by flowers floating on the surface of the paper rather than anchored in a composition. One distinctive example from this period is *Red and Yellow Gladioli* (Plate 38).

In 1928 Demuth was exhibited at the Twenty-seventh International Exhibition, Carnegie Institute, Pittsburgh, and he had his second one-man show at the Intimate Gallery. It was indeed a banner year for Demuth. Not only did he create some of his loveliest florals and figure work, but also his two portrait poster masterpieces, *Longhi on Broadway* and most especially *I Saw the Figure 5 in Gold,* which is one of the most seminal works of American art from the first fifty years of this century.

The year 1929 was one of the last years that Charles Demuth devoted himself exclusively to still lifes and flower watercolors. He also had his first inclusion in the exhibition "Paintings by Nineteen Living Americans" at the Museum of Modern Art. Surely some of his best still lifes came at this time. For example, in *Green Pears* (Plate 39), one of Demuth's major works in this genre, the artist painted seven pears in a simple composition, stressing their radiant color and ripe fruit forms. He also painted such strange but wonderful combinations of vegetables and fruits as *Squashes and Red Apple* and *Red Cabbages, Rhubarb, and Orange.* Although he painted only five flower pictures during this year, they are considered to be some of his finest. They are *Calla Lilies, Kiss-Me-Over-the-Fence,* the superb *Red Poppies, Tulips,* and *Single Peonies.*

Even though these florals are more complex and lack the great simplicity of the still lifes, they still adhere to the same principles of structure. With the exception of *Kiss-Me-Over-the-Fence,* they all employ a single floral motif.

By 1930 Demuth began to work more on the oil and tempera paintings that support the idea that his work had qualities similar to the Precisionist mode of painting. Certainly the poster portraits are inspired by this hard-edged style. But because there are so few of these Precisionist-style paintings, they are atypical when compared to the main body of Demuth's work. Among Demuth's paintings that reflect this style are *Business; Pâquebot Paris; Modern Conveniences* (Plate 00); and *Nospmas M. Egiap Nospmas M.*, all of 1921; *My Egypt* (Plate 33), 1927; *Buildings—Lancaster* and *Waiting* (or *Ventilators*) in 1930; *". . . And the Home of the Brave!", Buildings Abstraction—Lancaster,* and *Chimney and Water Tower,* all of 1931; none at all in 1932; only *"After all . . ."* in 1933; and none thereafter. These remain as a very small, but important part of Demuth's total working style.

THE WATERCOLORS Demuth painted in 1930 are stylistically very diverse. They include one of the artist's rare book illustrations, *Distinguished Air* (Figure 14), which is Demuth's idea of a composite scene that conveys the essence of the book. Its inscription, "For 'Distinguished Air' by Robert McAlmon," suggests that it was not meant to depict actual events in the book, but was more likely to reveal the book's outlook. In the watercolor, two women and three men

Figure 14. DISTINGUISHED AIR, *1930.*
Illustration for Robert McAlmon's book of the same name.
Watercolor and pencil on paper.
14 × 20 in. (25.6 × 50.8).
The Whitney Museum of American Art, New York.

are dressed in a variety of clothing. The man holding on to his sailor companion is wearing tails and high hat; the woman to his right is in a very décolleté evening gown, with a train, white gloves, a fan, and rhinestone buckles on her shoes. To their left is a less flamboyantly dressed couple—the woman staring intently at the statue of *Princess X*, by Brancusi, while her derby-hatted friend leers equally intently at the sailor. Above the statue is a painting of a beach scene. The *Princess X* is placed on a three-level stand that echoes the sailor's collar. Only the center of the watercolor is painted. The rest of the picture is drawn in the fine line typical of the artist.

The year 1930 was the last year Demuth did his so-called "pornographic" works, many of French sailors. Apparently, the remainder of his total work in this genre was done on order for Professor Darrell Larsen, a Lancaster friend and teacher. They became friends and later traveled together to Provincetown and Newport.

Like all of the later years of the artist's life, 1931 shows a greatly diminished output attributed, most assuredly, to his failing health and energies. It was only in Lancaster, where his mother took care of him, that Demuth was able to work. She saw to it that her son took the proper medication and ate the prescribed kind of food. When Charles was away from home, he paid little or no attention to these vital matters of his health. It was undoubtedly the reason for the lessening output of work, which diminished measurably during the last five years of his life.

Despite his failing health, however, Demuth's recognition continued to grow. In 1930 he was included in a group exhibition at

Stieglitz's An American Place Gallery and included in the Museum of Modern Art's exhibition "Retrospective." In 1931 he was represented for the first time at Edith Gregor Halpert's Downtown Gallery and again at An American Place Gallery. In 1932 he participated in the "Impromptu Exhibition of Selected Paintings" at An American Place Gallery and was included in "American Paintings and Sculpture (1862–1932)" at the Museum of Modern Art.

Demuth painted only four works in watercolor during 1932—all of them of French sailors. They are *Man and Sailors, On "That" Street, Sailors (and Girl),* and *Sailors with Douglas Sommerville.* These paintings are similiar to the sailors and nudes of 1930, but are far less sexually explicit. All total, it remains an odd year for Demuth, who was suffering from diabetic fatigue.

FORTUNATELY, the next two years were much more productive ones for Demuth. In 1933 his work included one landscape oil, *"After All . . .",* two lovely still lifes, and some of his finest watercolors of flowers. He also exhibited in the first "Biennial Exhibition of Contemporary American Painting" at the Whitney Museum of American Art. These paintings are among the last works of Charles Demuth.

In 1934, at the urging of his mother and his good friends from Lancaster, Frank and Elsie Everts, Demuth spent part of the summer at Provincetown. He reverted to his figure works, even painting beach scenes similar to those he did in 1915. These works, although similar in genre, are enormously different

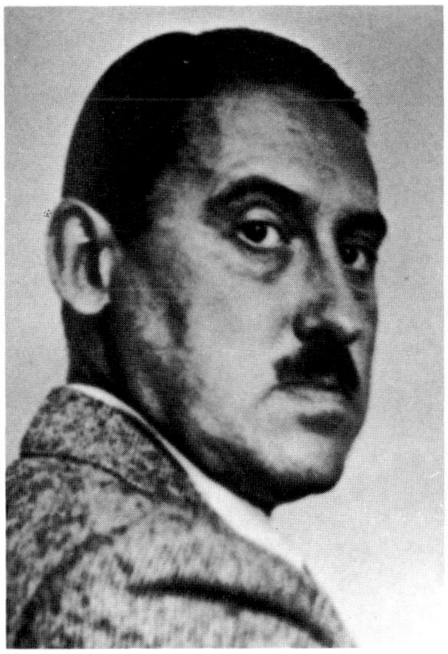

*Figure 15. 1932 photograph
of Charles Demuth
taken by Dorothy Norman.*

from the early watercolors. They were executed right on the spot, first briefly sketched in pencil and then watercolored, often very incompletely. They are far simpler than the early beach scenes but are technically more complex. All of the figures are basically silhouettes, and here and there are glimpses of water, sand, children's buckets, hats, and the usual paraphernalia found on beaches. Another interesting difference between these and the earlier beach scenes is the quality of the skin color—the obvious 1934 attempt to get a fine tan was quite the opposite notion of some twenty years before.

Demuth did not lose his touch as a draftsman in these last works. Some scenes held enough interest for him so that he would do two or three studies of the same one. In *Beach Study, Provincetown,* as in all of these, there exists a wit and humor, a feeling of joyousness in being with caring friends in one of his most cherished places and doing what he liked best—creating and enjoying the sights he had not viewed for four years. The pleasure the artist received is palpable in these works, as in the truly exceptional *Man and Woman, Provincetown* (Plate 40), where the muted browns and gray-blacks of the two pedestrians walking their dog give added weight to their ponderous bodies. Only the dog and the pier pole help to balance the strong forms of the onlooking couple, fully attired for the beach.

In 1934 Charles Demuth was among the artists in the "Nineteenth International Biennale Art Exhibition" in Venice, Italy, and was also in "Five Americans" at the Smith College Museum of Art. Most of the year, however, was spent in Lancaster, with very occasional railroad journeys to Philadelphia and New York.

He may have worked on some of the beach scenes from Provincetown, those watercolors he painted in 1934, but there are no works at all from 1935.

On October 23, 1935, returning from New York on the train, he fell into a diabetic coma and was taken to 118 East King Street in Lancaster, where he died in his own bedroom.

CHARLES Demuth was a well-built man despite his lameness. He had an olive complexion, with brown eyes and dark hair, and a bit of a cast in one eye. He was elegant, self-confident, well read, and had literary tastes that were advanced for the time.

Demuth's relationship with Robert Locher was an example of his devout loyalty and complete discreetness. Although the relationship was known in Lancaster, it was seldom if ever discussed. Augusta Demuth was fond of Bobby Locher, and she agreed to go along with her son's wishes to leave the house on East King Street, its furnishings, and most of Demuth's paintings to him. The remainder of the paintings—the temperas and oils—went to Georgia O'Keeffe.

After Mrs. Demuth's death in 1943, Robert Locher moved from New York back to Lancaster with his friend Richard C. Weyand. They turned the downstairs of the Demuth home into a gift and antique shop, where Locher sold Demuth paintings whenever a collector wanted one or whenever he needed money. When Locher died in 1956 he willed everything, including the Demuth home and the remaining Demuth paintings, to Richard Weyand.

At Weyand's death the same year, five months after Locher, his inheritance was left intestate. His four siblings all shared one-quarter of their brother's estate. They then sold the house to a real estate firm and put the most valuable or most finished of Demuth's works up for sale. But it was not until 1970 that the last drawings and watercolors were distributed by lot to the four brothers and sisters. These works have either been exhibited and sold, auctioned off, or in some instances destroyed!

THE REPRODUCTIONS of Charles Demuth's work that are illustrated in this volume demonstrate with great clarity that placing this artist in any one school or style does him a great injustice. His wit and humor were not just a family trait but inherent in his work from 1895. His versatility in so many of the forms of painting leaves far behind many of his fellow artists.

Charles Demuth, John Marin, and to a lesser degree Georgia O'Keeffe were the innovators of the watercolor medium from the 1920s on. They took this most difficult medium, which had been almost reserved for the works of amateurs and decorators, and made it into the means of a new aesthetic. Maurice Prendergast, though somewhat earlier, was also very much a creator of his own watercolor method and style and can be included in this list of American watercolor masters of the twentieth century.

Among these four, however, Demuth stands out because he never let his technique interfere with new discoveries in style, although his approach to watercolor changed immensely in the forty years he worked in this medium, from the sensuous and explosive florals of the early years to the almost Chinese delicacy and subtlety of the later works. Demuth's possibly apocryphal statement regarding the differences in his and Marin's approach is worth noting.

All of us drew our inspiration from the spring of French modernism. John Marin pulled his up by the bucketfuls but he spilled much along the way. I had only a teaspoon in which to carry mine; but I never spilled a drop.[6]

There is certainly an element of truth in this, but still more important is Demuth's constant effort to move ahead and to refine and even change a style when it did not suit the genre or his aesthetic development.

FROM HIS adolescence on, if not earlier, Charles Demuth showed a great independence. Even in his student days at the Pennsylvania Academy of Fine Arts, he had strong opinions and was resistant to the influences of his teachers and the painting styles influential at the time.

Years later in his Bermuda landscapes, which were a long stride forward in his approach to painting, Demuth accepted the Cubist precepts of Gleizes and Metzinger. His series of trees reflected the Pennsylvania artist's own inquiry into the structure of arboreal forms. This attachment to the composition and discovery of the "bare-bones," the skeleton that lies behind trees, rooftops, flowers, foliage, landscapes, seascapes, dunes, is what is essentially Charles Demuth. It is also part of what is important about Georgia O'Keeffe and

Figure 16. SPRING, *c. 1921.*
Oil on academy board.
21¾ × 23¾ in. (55.3 × 60.3 cm).
Hirschl & Adler Galleries, Inc., New York.
Swatches of cloth signaling
the arrival of spring.

John Marin—a search for the basic element behind the subject matter. *Dunes, Provincetown, Bermuda, Dancing Sailors* (Plate 13), and *Red Chimneys* (Plate 17), are just a few examples of Demuth's discoveries in watercolor.

Demuth's works in tempera from 1919 on are also innovative in their use of faceting, in their titles, and in the artist's use of buildings as compositional structures. Such works as *A Sky After El Greco, Box of Tricks* (Plate 23), and *Backdrop of East Lynne* illustrate this next phase in Demuth's versatility.

The many oils, temperas, and studies for the poster portraits still remain the most innovative of all of Demuth's genre. It is interesting that not one of these ever sold in his lifetime. It is unfortunate that the portraits for Marsden Hartley and Wallace Stevens were never completed and the portrait for Marcel Duchamp has never been discovered. These homages are all important developments in international art. It is possible to seek and even find some slight evidences of feasible influences from a Marsden Hartley, from Alexandre Cassandre, from the analytical Cubism of Picasso and Braque, or even from Stuart Davis, but basically the portraits are the very original and private efforts of Demuth.

The development of Demuth's still lifes parallels the artist's aesthetic development, from his early works to the final years. But attempting to categorize them into different styles of still lifes, such as "figure-eights" or "amorphous, wet" is not possible. Demuth certainly moved from the soft-edge to the hard, as did so many of the artists who followed him, but even this factor is not that consistent in his work.

T is difficult to understand why many critics have categorized Demuth's work with that of the Precisionists, because only approximately twenty of his works are painted in that style. All of his work up through 1920 falls far more into a late development of his Bermuda and Provincetown style, with only a slight tendency toward the faceting of forms. Demuth was surely influenced by Cubism, but perhaps more importantly by the running stream of Dada. It is only after his last European trip that anything like the abstract quality of Precisionism can be applied to Demuth's work. Some of his paintings, such as *Modern Conveniences* (Plate 27); *Machinery; Stairway, Provincetown; Business;* and *Spring* (Figure 16) all have different starting concepts, often based on Picabia and Duchamp, but even more they reflect Demuth's frown upon his changing world. *Incense of a New Church, Aucassin and Nicolette, Red State of the Grey Church, Nospmas M. Egiap Nospmas M., After Sir Christopher Wren* (or *New England*), *The Tower* (or *After Sir Christopher Wren*) all arise from this concept of a fragmented world, the new being less good than the old. Others such as *Buildings* (Plate 24), *My Egypt* (Plate 33), *Paquebot Paris, Chimney and Water Tower, Waiting* (or *Ventilators*), "*. . . And the Home of the Brave,*" and "*After All . . .*" do come closer to Precisionism, but they remain quite apart from the works of other Precisionists like Charles Sheeler, Ralston Crawford, Niles Spencer, and Stuart Davis. Their creative impulses spring from other sources.

The artistic element that Charles Demuth did share with Precisionism was his sense of

Figure 17. Church steeple in Lancaster that can be seen from the Demuth home. It is the inspiration for several of the architectural landscapes.

composition or structure. In *My Egypt* (Plate 33), as was his custom, the base is dominant and dark-toned, and the diagonal rays are balanced by strong horizontal and vertical lines. All of his works, which were always based on real subjects and places Demuth knew, have an imaginative quality that takes them away from the photographic and places them into a magical, monumental world. *"After All . . ."* and especially *". . . And the Home of the Brave!"* the last two architectural works by Demuth, share this enchanting and monumental feeling of wizardry.

DEMUTH wrote for several literary and artistic magazines and publications, such as *Creative Art, The Glebe, The Dial, Camera Work, Manuscripts, The Little Review, Rogue, The Blind Man,* as well as for the *Lancaster County Historical Society Papers.* He also wrote a fine introduction to one of Georgia O'Keeffe's exhibitions at The Intimate Gallery and a foreword to a Peggy Bacon show at the same gallery.

The strong regard that fellow artists had for Demuth is best shown by the many writings about him by various artists of the time. In *A Tribute to the Artist* Marcel Duchamp wrote:

He had a very curious smile reflecting an incessant curiosity for every manifestation life offered.

An artist worthy of the name, without the pettiness which afflicts most artists; worshipping his inner self without the usual eagerness to be right.

Demuth was also one of the few artists whom all other artists liked as a real friend, a rare case indeed.

His work is a living illustration of the disappearance of a "Monroe Doctrine" applied to Art; for today, art is no more the crop of privileged soils, and Demuth is among the first to have planted the good seed in America.[7]

William Carlos Williams dedicated his book of poetry *Spring and All* to Charles Demuth.

petals radiant with piercing light
contending
    above
the leaves
reaching up their modest green
from the pot's rim . . .[8]

Marsden Hartley wrote in *The New Caravan,* "Farewell, Charles."

Summer was on the way to being over, he [Demuth] booked passage home to begin the scientific experiments with the now so famous insulin treatments, . . . it let him live fifteen years longer than he assumed he could . . . he never knew when he would be overtaken with those violent and terrifying collapses,

. . . He was a bit Proustian . . . he liked fragile gossip, he liked the flare of à la mode emotions, he liked superficialities, but with the difference that being a serious person, he understood the vast implications of the little secrets of life.

Charles's hands were unusual, and some of us will miss them, how the Chinese would have feted them, even Charles's whole appearance was at times permeated with oriental stillness . . .

. . . he had a capacity for admiration as well as friendship, he believed in friends, and was amply supplied with them, a nice old-fashioned quality . . .

As for his works of art, they attest to themselves, they are always in the best of taste, conscious of good tradition . . . perhaps too concrete an insistence upon the elements of refinement and grace . . .

Charles never made a bad picture . . . He knew the laws of picture making, and that is something that not all painters know . . . The transition from the earlier, superior illustrative subjects to the later, cubistically evolved realistic pictures, is all one thing, and there is, therefore, a natural sequence in the product . . .

Charles loved the language of paint with the fervour of an ardent linguist . . .

Charles traversed the all in all thin area of esthetic experience with a firm step, and he left footprints here and there which have long since been measured and found of the proper size.[9]

ENRY McBride, the renowned art critic for *The New York Herald* and *The New York Evening Sun*, became a friend to both Charles and Augusta. He visited Lancaster often and was a welcome guest at their house, eventually becoming a beneficiary of the Demuth estate. His evaluation of his artist-friend increased in its critical validity as McBride's anti-avant-garde prejudices and the problems he found in Cubism became clearer.

> Charles Demuth, whose watercolors are on view at the Daniel Gallery . . . loves a certain bay, with green shores and blue water and rainbow skies. He has painted it over and over again . . . They are stamped with authenticity of affection. They are rich in color delight.[10]

> There are some watercolors that have not been hung on the walls. The subjects were suggested by reading of Zola's *Nana*. They are kept hidden in a portfolio, and are shown to museum directors and proved lovers of modern art upon presentation of visiting cards. They are quite advanced in style. . . .

> When the flower pictures had already made Demuth known, and it had become fashionable to own one, Mr. Daniel, who was then Mr. Demuth's merchant, showed us all, surreptitiously, some figure drawings. They were not precisely shocking, but one or two of the drawings illustrated points in Zola's *Nana*, and just before the war we were sufficiently Victorian to shudder at the thought of exposing pictures of reprehensible *Nana* on the walls . . . Times, of course, have greatly changed since then and now "Nana," poor dear, can go anywhere she wants to, but by the time our collectors had realized that "Nanas" had become perfectly all right, and rather better company than most, the entire lot of Mr. Demuth's figure drawings had been swept into some specially well-hidden collection, and it was announced that the artist was not to do any more figures![11]

> He grows more earnest and eloquent with the times; . . . but he also grows more aesthetic. His studies of aspects of New England and Pennsylvania would be quite terrible—if they were not so beau-

tiful. Whether he has studied Nietzsche or not I do not know, but he certainly sees plenty of applied Nietzscheanism in this beloved but hard country of ours. Mr. Demuth must have gone through the period of terror into which most sensitive artists plunge upon returning to this country from the *dolce far niente* of the Paris school days . . .[12]

The change from the warm, perfumed atmosphere of the "Nana" drawings to the chill of the "Coatesville Steel Mills" . . . is remarkable.[13]

REMARKS such as these demonstrate the disparity of ideas and opinions, which are sometimes based on each individual critic's self-concept. The alteration in the views of Henry McBride shows that he, unlike some other critics, could change with the times and learn from artists such as Charles Demuth.

Alfred Stieglitz and his galleries were of great value and influence to Demuth, long before he became part of the Stieglitz conclave. It was here that he saw works by Picasso, Matisse, Rodin, Cézanne, and many others. More important was Demuth's ability to communicate with Stieglitz. In Demuth's article called "Between Four and Five" for *Camera Work* is his answer to "What is 291?"

The forenoon has been this and that.

The afternoon dragged through an exhibition or two, a saloon or two—some art talk.

Then, somehow—tired and discouraged, we found ourselves at Fisk's suggestion, at a place, a gallery, that, I like the word place better than the word gallery, for this place.

"May I see the new Picasso?"

It was brought into the room. A Picasso.

That was a moment.

"What does it mean? It was a moment."

Again the forenoon had been this and that. Again the afternoon had been given to this and that—had been wasted.

"Let us go in here"—and we went in again to the place which is more than a gallery—just a place in movement; just— rather one of the few.

The walls this time were hung, emotionally with African carvings—there was also yellow and orange and black; yellow, orange, black.

There were photographs of African carvings. There was a photograph of two hands.

That was a moment.

"Let us start a magazine—a gallery, a theatre." This is always in the air; seldom: "Let me create a moment."[14]

Here is another Demuth quote on the subject of aesthetics.

Paintings must be looked at and looked at and looked at—they (the good ones) like it. They must be understood, and that's not the work either, through the eyes. No writing, no singing, no dancing will explain them. They are the final, the *nth* whoopee of sight. A watermelon, a kiss may be fair, but after all have other uses. "Look at that!" is all that can be said

before a great painting, at least by those that really see it.[15]

It is easy to understand the empathy between Stieglitz and Demuth, and although there was never any financial arrangement between them, there was much admiration and respect. It can be regretted that not even a poster portrait was done for Stieglitz, but it is more than possible that the artist felt there was too much to include, or that such a homage was just not enough.

DESPITE the attributions of the saloons, Turkish-baths, and massage parlors, Demuth seems to have kept himself discreet and always maintained that his work was the most important aspect of his life.

The words "decadent" or "perverse," ascribed to Demuth because of his predilection for such haunts as the Red Parrot, the Golden Swan, and the Purple Pup, or for illustrating such works as *Nana* and *Pandora*, should by now have been forever laid to rest. Unfortunately, there are still far too many critiques of his work that are based completely on Demuth's sexual preferences and his drinking during Prohibition.

Such works as *Man with Book, Strolling*, or the even more pertinent *On Stage* (Figure 4) and *Marshall's* (Plate 6) all demonstrate Demuth's astounding ability to capture the characters that caught his eye. His empathy for performers and people of all sorts in a bar or on the street or resting or playing on the beach gave the impetus to his drawings and watercolors of acrobats, dancers, and circus performers. In these scenes there are no ele-

ments of sex or perversion, even though too many early critics perceived them as such. Demuth's sensitivity to color, to the struggles of the performers to please their audience, to the composition of his paintings, and to the fluidity of his line are the most important factors of his oeuvre.

It was Demuth's sense of fantasy, his ability to perceive enigmas in reality, and his joy in not only the human form but in the shapes of trees, houses, flora, that differentiate his work from all others. Even those of his works which tend to be closest to Precisionism move in and out of the paper with the same skill and sense of the surreal that make the still lifes and flower watercolors evanesce.

From the illustrations for *Nana* through those for the Wedekind plays, the two James tales, and the last "*For McAlmon's Distinguished Air,*" Demuth gave his special qualities of acute perception and consuming interest. Other artists were as empathetic to their subject as Demuth, and others were almost as versatile, but in his masterpieces, the illustrations for *The Beast in the Jungle* and *The Turn of the Screw*, Demuth set standards that have rarely been achieved by other artists.

NEW YORK was a very special place during and immediately after World War I and throughout the era of Prohibition. During this period there was a great influx of artists coming to New York, people unaccustomed to racial discrimination who appreciated the sounds and the fervor of black jazz and music. They introduced Demuth to a new world of delights. It was at Marshall's that Demuth received the inspiration for five of his most impressive figure paintings. These paintings are simply called *At Marshall's*, one from 1915 and the other 1917; and another called *Marshall's* (Plate 6), 1915. In these memorable watercolors Demuth captured the spirit of the Harlem jazz speakeasies. There is absolutely no element of slumming or of snobbery, but an artist's joy in the music.

In those days of discovery—the new music and new art—there was an overall give and take, a participation among the artists, musicians, playwrights, actors, writers, poets, sculptors, and photographers as never before. Because of the tragedy of World War I, the influx of European ideas coming to America and the impact of the controversial Armory Show there was a great sense of excitement in America, as well as a sense of doom.

CHARLES Demuth's versatility as an artist, his ability to develop his own unique style and leave behind Fauvism, Synchronism, Futurism, and the other new waves of the prewar years, are unexcelled. It is as easy to identify a Demuth painting as it is to distinguish an O'Keeffe, a Marin, or a Dove, but there is a far greater variety and sense of experimentation in the Lancastrian.

The high-pitched roofs of Lancaster, the Wrenlike steeples, the backyard gardens, the Pennsylvania-Dutch insistence on privacy were all part of Charles Demuth's inheritance. He memorialized this in temperas and oils showing the changing landscapes of the places he lived, not only in Lancaster but in Provincetown and Gloucester as well. In his New England works the masts of ships became the antennae of the radio towers of Lancaster.

Like his friend Georgia O'Keeffe, Demuth's love of nature eventually made his mother's garden and the fruit and vegetables from the Lancaster markets vital to him. His last journey to Provincetown in 1934 showed his deftness and his fine draftsmanship at its peak, as did the florals of 1933. It was only the state of Demuth's frail health and his absolute inability to look out for himself that lowered his impulses toward creation, but never his basic development to ever greater creativity and purity. His standards for himself were always steady in his search for imagination and artistic growth.

NOTES

1. James Johnson Sweeney, *Stuart Davis*, The Museum of Modern Art, New York, 1945.

2. Letter to Alfred Stieglitz from Charles Demuth, Fall 1921. Collection of American Literature. Beinecke Rare Book and Manuscript Library. Yale University.

3. Marsden Hartley, "Farewell, Charles, An Outline in Portraiture of Charles Demuth—Painter," in *The New Caravan*, edited by Alfred Kreymborg, Lewis Mumford, and Paul Rosenfeld. W.W. Norton and Co., New York, 1936.

4. Charles Demuth, "Introduction to Georgia O'Keeffe's Paintings," The Intimate Gallery, 1927.

5. William Carlos Williams, "The Great Figure," *Collected Earlier Poems*. Copyright 1938 by New Directions Publishing Corporation. Reprinted by permission of New Directions.

6. George Biddle, *An American Artist's Story*, Little, Brown and Co., Boston, 1939.

7. Marcel Duchamp, "A Tribute to the Artist," in Andrew C. Ritchie, *Charles Demuth*, The Museum of Modern Art, New York, 1950.

8. William Carlos Williams, "The Pot of Flowers," *Collected Earlier Poems*, Copyright 1938 by New Directions Publishing Corporation. Reprinted by permission of New Directions.

9. Marsden Hartley, "Farewell, Charles, An Outline in Portraiture of Charles Demuth—Painter," in *The New Caravan*, edited by Alfred Kreymborg, Lewis Mumford, and Paul Rosenfeld, W.W. Norton and Co., 1936.

10. Henry McBride, *The New York Sun*, October 30, 1914.

11. ———, *The New York Evening Sun*, November 25, 1917.

12. ———, "Watercolors by Charles Demuth," in *Creative Art*, September 1929.

13. ———, *The New York Sun*, December 5, 1920.

14. Charles Demuth, "Between Four and Five," in *Camera Work*, July 1914.

15. William Murrell, *Charles Demuth*, Whitney Museum of American Art, 1945.

Color Plates

Plate 1 (bottom, left)
SPRING CLOUDS

This early watercolor was given to Ann Locher by her uncle, Robert Locher, as a birthday gift, after he had inherited Demuth's watercolors. The Locher-Schroeder family (Locher's nieces and nephews) were told that *Spring Clouds* had been painted in 1899, when Demuth was sixteen, and not in 1912–14, as it had previously been dated. It is, indeed, very different from these latter works, as it possesses both a tenderness and youthfulness that is lacking in the Fauve-influenced oils and watercolors painted during the pre-War years. Although the brushstrokes of the foreground are quite bold, the fine lines of the trees and foliage soften this characteristic and give it the delicacy of Pennsylvania farmland in the spring.

This early landscape may have been a sketch for one of Demuth's art classes; it has a feeling for the soil and the Pennsylvania countryside that one would hardly believe of the later sophisticated and elegant Demuth. The milky blue-white clouds, which give the painting its title, and the soft reddish color of the horizon blend with the burgeoning green of the leaves, evoking springtime in the farmlands near Lancaster.

c. 1899. Watercolor on paper,
9 × 12 in. (22.8 × 30.4 cm).
Private collection.

Plate 2 (top, left)
COASTAL SCENE *or* ÉTRETAT

Demuth executed a group of watercolors between 1912 and 1915 with such titles as *Inlet, Provincetown, Bay #1, #2, #3*, and so forth plus *Early Landscape*. Most of these depict the bay of Étretat, with boats moored on the sand; others were of Provincetown. In this work, probably the finest of the group, Demuth painted both the verdant cliffs that come down to the sand and the village in the background in a manner close to that of the Fauves in its depth of color and broad brush strokes. In contrast to the works of 1916 and after, *Coastal Scene* has a looseness to it; yet Demuth's strong palette and sense of control keep the structural components clear.

The predominance of green relates each section of the work to its counterpart; Demuth uses the deepest tones of each color as a kind of artistic shorthand to delineate the trees, houses, moored boats, sea, and cliffs. *Coastal Scene* is far more contemporary in its vision than other early works and seems to point forward to Demuth's later work.

c. 1912. Watercolor on paper,
9⅞ × 12⅞ in. (25.1 × 32.7 cm).
Private collection.

Plate 3
HOUSETOPS, SEASHORE

Together with some figure watercolors, *Housetops, Seashore* demonstrates a freedom and mastery of the watercolor medium that hardly exists in Demuth's later works or even in the beach scenes. The painting appears to be of Provincetown, with the bay in the background. The colors are applied wet, almost in the manner of Paul Klee. Roofs, trees, windows, and shoreline are treated with controlled washes; only pencil lines delineate the forms. The warm, reddish-brown colors of the houses in the left foreground are echoed in the sand and shoreline; and the soft greens of the pine trees extend down into the trees below them and from there to the lightly washed greens of the houses and roofs in the right foreground. Gray hues, from light to dark and from blue-gray to mauve, move throughout the composition and unify its structure. The watercolor has a whimsical and delicate wit that appears in different form in subsequent, and more concisely conceived works; but *Housetops, Seashore* has an ephemeral beauty that is unique.

1912. Watercolor on paper,
8½ × 11 in. (21.6 × 27.9 cm).
Private collection.

Plate 4 (right)
FLOWER PIECE

This fascinating watercolor is like an explosion of fireworks bursting toward the sky. Within the cataclysm one can see daisies, blue hyacinths, red sage, and Queen Anne's lace. The paper, as in all of Demuth's works of this time, is completely covered with the watercolor wash. Even in these early florals Demuth was innovative. The paper was undoubtedly dampened before the paint was applied, and although this can at times result in happy accidents, it appears here as if Demuth conceived every brushstroke before his brush touched the paper. The forms are outlined as well as created by the wash, but it is the quality of the brushstrokes that make *Flower Piece* so original to Demuth at this period in his career. Throughout the painting, color is applied in short brushstrokes. The one exception to this rather impressionistic style appears at the upper right where longer brushstrokes are used, giving the effect of flowers erupting into mid-air.

The exuberance of *Flower Piece* is a delight to behold. One can just picture the artist lying in a field of spring flowers with his head on the fertile ground. Here the hyacinths, violets, and an entire multitude of flowers appear to be moving toward the sun and sky. It is this feeling of movement and joy and beauty that Charles Demuth perceived and painted in the most heady period of his life and artistry.

1915. Watercolor on paper,
18 × 11½ in. (45.7 × 29.2 cm).
Williams College Museum of Art,
Williamstown, Massachusetts.

Plate 5 (far right)
ALLOVER PATTERN OF LILACS

Until 1916, Demuth's floral watercolors typically covered the entire paper, and all were slightly explosive, as if the flowers were skyrocketing. Of these early florals, however, *Allover Pattern of Lilacs* is the most delicate. Although Demuth painted several watercolors of lilacs, this is one of the most successful attempts. The challenge of this particular flower—consisting of many florets, all of which have within them many shades of lilac—has been superbly met, and at the same time the artist has managed to avoid undue sweetness.

It is characteristic of Demuth's floral works that no flower or branch ever droops. Instead, each flower and stem is erect and firm, moving up toward the sun. The subtle tones of mauve, lavender, and lilac in the florets are balanced by the cool greens in the leaves. The painter has given his subject the careful scrutiny of a bee in the bush, closely examining each leaf and flower.

c. 1915. Watercolor on paper,
18 × 12 in. (45.7 × 30.5 cm).
The Canton Art Institute, Canton, Ohio.

Plate 6 (right)
MARSHALL'S

Marshall's was a New York City nightclub that featured black performers. Located beneath the Sixth Avenue elevated train, it was frequented not only by Demuth but by the art critic Henry McBride, the artist Florine Stettheimer, and the novelist and music critic Carl Van Vechten, among others. It is obvious that this was a favorite haunt of Demuth's as there are several other works that were inspired by this nightclub. They include *At Marshall's*, *Negro Singer*, and *Negro Jazz Band*, as well as another *Marshall's* painted the following year. In all of these paintings, the artist has achieved a steaminess and intensity of performance typical of such bars and nightclubs in this New York jazz era. One can almost feel the closeness of the performers to the patrons in this pre-Prohibition bar where such famous jazz personalities as Florence Dunbar and Bill Bailey appeared.

The overall color of reddish brown permeates the entire background of the watercolor, relieved here and there by light areas and some red and green swags above the piano player. A blue-haired person at a table repeats the color of the dancer's dress. The artist's pulsating pencil line is used extensively for the facial features, drums, bongo, music sheets, and other details. Marshall's is a tour-de-force illustration of a pre-World War I nightclub and of the early jazz era.

1915. Watercolor and pencil on paper,
13 × 8 in. (33 × 20.3 cm).
Courtesy of Kennedy Galleries, Inc., New York.

Plate 7 (far right)
IN VAUDEVILLE: THE GREEN DANCER

One of the finest and boldest of the *In Vaudeville* series, *The Green Dancer* uses one of Demuth's favorite themes—the twin, or reflected, spotlight. The large circular spotlight in the center illuminates each dancer, and the smaller, elliptical floor spot mainly lights the female dancer. Demuth focuses on the dancers themselves rather than the environment of the theater. Not even the stage floor is apparent here, except in the intense area of light just above the floor spotlight; the rest of the stage dissolves into the mottled, sepia tones of the backdrop.

Like most of his watercolors of this period, Demuth completely covers the paper with transparent washes and defines the figures with his delicate pencil line. This wash and pencil effect is most effectively combined in the female figure. The girl's filmy short gown, created by light washes, reveals her form underneath. The dress's draped sleeves have brown, satiny cuffs with a translucent green lining.

A luxurious sense of color and form pervades these dancers. *The Green Dancer* is an apex in one of Demuth's most creative years.

1916. Watercolor and pencil on paper,
11 × 8 in. (27.9 × 20.3 cm).
The Philadelphia Museum of Art:
The Samuel S. White III
and Vera White Collection.

Plate 8

NANA, SEATED LEFT, AND SATIN AT LAURE'S RESTAURANT

This illustration for Zola's *Nana* is one of a series that Demuth worked on from 1916 to 1918. He also did illustrations for Wedekind's *Erdgeist, Pandora's Box*, and *Lulu*; for Poe's *The Masque of the Red Death*; as well as for Zola's *Assommoir*. In these, as well as his superb illustrations for Henry James's *The Beast in the Jungle* and *The Turn of the Screw*, Demuth completely covers the paper with a filmy watercolor wash and uses his loose, almost scribbled pencil lines to define the forms.

The acute angles of the tables, with their strangely deep perspective, give the viewer the sense of being elevated above the restaurant floor. The color, while handsome and apt, is limited to ochers and various shades of red, from coral to dark sepia tones. Here, Demuth uses color structurally to move from one part of the illustration to another, to balance and unify the composition. The two female figures in the center are far more prominent than any of the other figures, and the pitch of the tablecloth becomes the area that defines Nana and Satin and their belongings. The type of restaurant that Laure owns is indicated by the trio at the table to the left of Nana and by the pianist and singer to the right. The two men whose heads are centered between Nana and Satin appear to be Demuth and his friend Robert Locher.

Although these illustrations were handled by the Charles Daniel Gallery in New York, they were, according to critic Henry McBride "kept hidden in a portfolio, and are only shown to museum directors and proved lovers of modern art upon visitation of visiting cards . . . They were not precisely shocking, but one or two of the drawings illustrated points in Zola's *Nana*, and just before the War we were sufficiently Victorian to shudder at the thought of exposing pictures of reprehensible Nana on the walls. . . ." Today it is hard to imagine "shuddering" over Nana and Satin. Certainly it is astounding that these illustrations were shown surreptiously, but times do change, so that we can now take pleasure in their subtle, soft colors and charming lines.

Illustration for Emile Zola's Nana.
1916. Watercolor and pencil on paper,
8½ × 10¾ in. (21.6 × 27.3).
Collection: The Museum of Modern Art, New York.
Gift of Abby Aldrich Rockefeller.

Plate 9 (top, left)
TROPICAL PLANTS

This lovely tempera belongs with other works of this same year as *Cottage Window, Hanging Plants, Cineraria and Cyclamen, Calla Lilies, Still Life: Window With Plant,* and *The Primrose,* all oils or temperas. *Tropical Plants,* which was probably painted in Bermuda, has a tenderness and delicacy about it that is nonexistent in the others. This may be because *Tropical Plants* is the least influenced by Marsden Hartley. It does not use Hartley's typical window frame motif, and it is painted in a softer, more delicate style with far greater detail. A white primrose in the foreground of the painting is meticulously executed. This white flower becomes the focal point in the green foliage of the orange tree. Above this dense growth, a sturdier, more tropical-looking plant with oval-shaped leaves climbs upward and out of the painting.

There is a subtle assymetry to *Tropical Plants* which the artist has balanced by the thickness of the foreground foliage and by the triangle of oranges. The composition is comparatively intricate; the inverted pyramid of the primrose complements the triangle of fruit, all of which is enclosed by the larger tropical plant.

The palette is limited in *Tropical Plants.* Demuth used only the soft grays of the background, the orange of the fruit, the white of the primrose, and everything else is a myriad of wonderfully rich greens. The work seems to be the artist's reaction against the heavy impasto and bravura work of Hartley and an affirmation of his own more delicate approach.

c. 1916. Tempera on academy board,
14½ × 11½ in. (36.8 × 29.2 cm).
Private collection.

Plate 10 (bottom, left)
LANDSCAPE

During the years of World War I, Demuth's friend the artist Marsden Hartley was in Bermuda. Demuth joined him in late 1916, along with the artists Louis Bouché and Albert Gleizes. Demuth lived on this semi-tropical isle for almost half that year. During this time his work was very innovative and important to his aesthetic development. The change in Demuth's style is certainly obvious. In *Landscape* the imagination and stylization are completely new. For the first time Demuth uses color and forms to merely suggest objects like tree branches and leaves. Just as Demuth's pencil lines were a kind of shorthand in his figure watercolors, here patterns of color and shape describe the landscape. By this time Demuth had been to Europe twice, where he undoubtedly was exposed to not only the Impressionists, the Fauves, and the Blaue Reiter school but to early forms of Cubism as well. Since he was already acquainted with Cubism there is no sure way of knowing whether or not Charles Demuth was influenced by the Cubist styles of Hartley or Gleizes in Bermuda. In any case he was ready to alter his artistic concepts.

The composition moves from the dark branches at the top left of the paper, down to the center, and then back up to the right through a series of roofs, leaves, and water patterns. Serrations and repeated oval-shapes form the trees. In this work Demuth first used the blotter technique of watercolor. Here the color is applied in the customary wash technique but in order to make fine gradations and achieve a mottled texture, the excess paint is blotted and removed. This creates different values and textures within one color. *Landscape* has a delicacy and lightness unlike Demuth's previous work.

c. 1916. Watercolor on paper,
10 × 14 in. (25.4 × 35.6 cm).
The Denver Art Museum, Denver, Colorado.

Plate 11

THE CIRCUS

One of the most delightful of Demuth's vaudeville and circus series, *The Circus* has a vivaciousness and spontaneity that provide this watercolor with its charm. The subject matter may have been inspired by Degas or Toulouse-Lautrec, whose works Demuth must have seen in his trips to Paris, but the artist, as always, has perceived his subject from an intensely personal vision. The horse, painted in blotter technique, is almost invisible at the bottom of the painting and is executed in the most muted of tones. The tent pole with its multicolored banners reiterates the curvilinear forms of the acrobats.

The Circus portrays a scene of delicious elegance and gaiety. It focuses primarily on the male acrobat who has one foot on the horse and the other one raised up as he lifts his female partner high above his head. The green band around his chest echoes the color of one of the pole ribbons; similarly, his partner's apricot-colored hair matches the ribbon at the far left. The color of the circus ring is a slightly deeper tone of the coral-red tent pole. The elongated forms of the arms of the female acrobat and the legs of the male restate the curvilinear theme expressed in the curves of the ring and the draping ribbons.

1917. Watercolor on paper,
8 × 10⅜ in. (20.3 × 26.4 cm).
Columbus Museum of Art, Columbus, Ohio.
Gift of Ferdinand Howald.

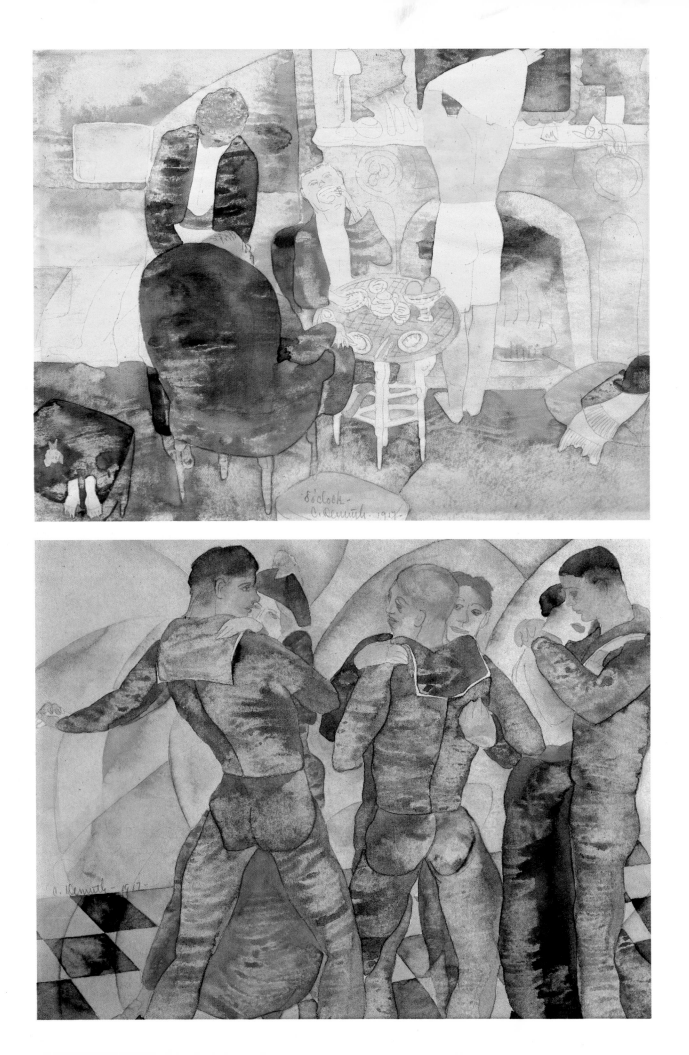

Plate 12 (top, left)
EIGHT O'CLOCK—EVENING

Eight O'Clock—Evening is one of a trio of works—
the other two are both entitled *Eight O'Clock—
Morning*—that were painted in 1917, the second
most prolific year of Demuth's career. In many
ways *Eight O'Clock—Evening* resembles *Dancing
Sailors* (1917), but it is much more illustrative. In
all three paintings three young men are preparing
for an evening on the town or are recovering from
the excesses of the previous evening. In this ver-
sion, two of the men are dining in their hotel room,
which is probably the Hotel Brevoort, where Demuth stayed during his visits to New York, while a
third man has just emerged from his bath and is
drying himself before the fireplace.

Demuth uses a combination of the wash-and-
blotter techniques to illustrate the men's belongings—a pair of gloves, a boutonniere, a white evening scarf, a derby hat—which are scattered around
the room, ready to be gathered up when the trio
goes out for the evening. The turned-down bed at
the left leads the eye into the room. Demuth has
concentrated most of the dark tones on this side of
the picture, using the derby, the dark of the fireplace, and the picture on the wall to unite the two
sides of the painting.

This work, as well as its companion pieces, bears
a close relationship to the *Nana* illustrations, with
an attention to detail that makes it almost a genre
work. Although nothing sexually explicit is happening in any of these paintings, there is an intimacy
that pervades them all.

*1917. Watercolor on paper,
8 × 10⅜ in. (20.3 × 26.3 cm).
Wadsworth Atheneum, Hartford, Connecticut.*

Plate 13 (bottom, left)
DANCING SAILORS

Demuth gave two different paintings this title, one
dated 1917 and the other 1918. The differences between the two versions are very slight, but the one
shown here has been less frequently reproduced.
The backgrounds are both curvilinear, and the
floors are a checkerboard, but figures in both pictures are identical. The male and female figures are
in the same positions, although here their anato-
mies are slightly more detailed.

Critics such as Henry McBride, Emily
Farnham, and others have often made too much of
Demuth's attraction to the so-called seedy side of
life—the cafes and bars he frequented, as well as
painted. The two central figures in both versions of
Dancing Sailors are sailors dancing together. Although this painting, with its homosexual over-
tones, was certainly a shocker in 1917, there were
no such places as USOs during World War I. Also,
it was not considered "nice" for a young girl to go
out with members of the armed forces during this
time except under very special conditions. It is
noteworthy that none of the "couples" seems to
find anything unusual with two men dancing together.

The texture throughout the watercolor has been
achieved through the blotter method. The composition is a triad formed by the three dancing couples. This watercolor possesses Charles Demuth's
delicacy, sense of humor, and wit.

*1917. Watercolor on paper,
7¾ × 9¾ in. (19.7 × 24.8 cm).
Courtesy of Kennedy Galleries, Inc., New York.*

Plate 14 (right)
ACROBATS

From 1916 through 1919, the acrobatic figures were a major theme of Demuth's. These paintings, some thirty-one watercolors, of jugglers, trapeze artists, tumblers, and acrobats comprise part of Demuth's *In Vaudeville* works. It is speculated that Demuth's interest in and admiration for these performers originated in his own lameness.

This superb example of the genre expresses Demuth's wonderment in the strength, agility, and balance of acrobats. The column created by the man standing on his hands, bearing his companion straight up upon his feet, serves as a vertical contrast to the clutter of hoops, and assorted props of their act. The dominant muted red color used for the tights of the acrobats makes the two figures the focal point of the composition. The vertical line created by the acrobats leans slightly toward the right and is balanced by the strong horizontal lines of the foreground.

The warm tawny colors, the earth tones, sepias, hennas, and yellows combined with Demuth's delicate pencil line creates the droll charm of *Acrobats*, 1917. One can easily imagine the pleasure Charles Demuth discovered in the tawdry backdrop of stars, the wonderful variety of objects, and the amazing contortions of the performers.

1917. Watercolor with pencil, mounted on board,
13 × 8 in. (33 × 20.3 cm).
Courtesy of Kennedy Galleries, Inc., New York.

Plate 15 (far right)
IN VAUDEVILLE: BIRD WOMAN

Charles Demuth was evidently fascinated with this bird woman, whom he had seen either at a circus appearing locally or more probably at a vaudeville act in one of the two Lancaster theaters. He did two other watercolors on the same theme, *Circus Woman with Birds*, which is almost identical to this painting, and the *Aviariste*. All of these paintings are of a rather portly woman in a low-cut blue satin evening gown who is surrounded by several trained parrots. *In Vaudeville: Bird Woman*, the woman holds a red parrot on her left hand and a blue-white bird on her upraised right hand. Sitting on the table to the left is a small gray parrot perched on two two rings. A gray and yellow-breasted bird sits on the lower hoop. On the dressing table is a small chariot device with tennis balls for wheels, supposedly in which one bird rides while another pulls it.

With the exception of the table, the design of the watercolor is almost completely curvilinear: the circular yellow spotlight, the hoops and rings, and the round, buxom figure and curly blond hair of the woman. The washes and streaks of intense color combine with Demuth's loose, delicate pencil lines to give the painting its depth and definition. Demuth has captured here not only the vibrancy of the act but the coyness and corniness of it as well.

1917. Watercolor and pencil on paper,
11½ × 9¼ in. (29.2 × 23.5 cm).
Courtesy of Kennedy Galleries, Inc., New York.

Plate 16 (top, left)
RED-ROOFED HOUSES

This watercolor of the Bermuda series can be called a study in comparative Cubism. Here Demuth uses texture as an essential part of the composition which is far more prismatic and less varied in color than is, for example, *Bermuda*. It is limited to grayed blues, ochers, and tans, with just one area of red on the roofs. The values, however, are more varied, moving from almost pure white to near black. The blotter method is used to give texture to the forms and to define them at the same time. The artist has added a kind of grid pattern which gives additional definition to the roofs and sides of the houses.

A Red-Roofed House contains, despite its small size, boundless subtleties of color and character. A chimney at the upper left seems to evaporate from a mottled, shell-pink color into the air. Tree branches, as well as roofs, windows, and walls move in and out of one another and then disappear. Although *A Red-Roofed House* may when first seen appear to be a jumble of roofs and houses, its basic simplicity and structure become clearer with each fresh viewing.

c. 1917. Watercolor on paper,
10 × 14 in. (25.4 × 36.8 cm).
The Philadelphia Museum of Art:
The Samuel S. White III
and Vera White Collection.

Plate 17 (bottom, left)
RED CHIMNEYS

This work originated in Demuth's adoption of Cubism into his own aesthetic and in the great advance of his technical abilities. Painted in Provincetown, it is one of the loveliest of a series of rooftop and chimney works of 1918. The color here is more subdued than usual, moving from cold grays to warm mauvish tones and from Vandyke browns to the reds of the chimneys. The chimneys, which are like stepping stones, and the roofs and branches are all concentrated in the center of the painting, with a roof line on either side to frame the work like a proscenium. In this watercolor Demuth's mastery of his medium is superb. His use of line, whether penciled or brushed, is unexcelled as it defines and outlines roofs, buildings, windows, branches, foliage, and the red chimneys. It is noteworthy that when Demuth chose one of his paintings as a gift for Gertrude Stein, he chose one of this series. Miss Stein was most pleased with it.

The overall design of the painting is rectilinear and triangular. The branches and the slightest hint of leaves combine to move the design upward, enclosing the most prominent chimney in the center. Demuth uses the chessboardlike textures to soften the angular severity of New England houses. *Red Chimneys* is a pure and lovely example of Demuth's Cubist inspired landscapes.

1918. Watercolor and pencil on paper,
9¾ × 13¾ in. (24.8 × 34.9 cm).
The Phillips Collection, Washington, D.C.

Plate 18
IN VAUDEVILLE: DANCER WITH CHORUS

Exuberance is the key to this carefully thought-out watercolor of the halcyon days of local vaudeville shows during and after World War I. It is most likely that *In Vaudeville: Dancer with Chorus* was sketched at one of the two Lancaster theaters because the rather small chorus is indicative of a small town stage.

The technique employed here is a combination of wash and blotter. The total effect is one of exuberance for and a joy in the performance of the dancers. The tuxedo-clad figure of the male dancer is by far the most prominent, and the four female figures of the chorus provide a colorful backdrop to him within the main spotlight. In this painting Demuth has solved the problems of a rectangular "canvas" by using a full circle for its center, another concentric circle below it, and an oval shape above in the backdrop. In fact, these "spotlights" are contrived by the artist because they are not really illuminating anything.

Demuth has unified this watercolor by using colors that are closely related and by tones and tints of the same color. Even the black of the dancer's tuxedo has brown tonalities which unify him with the background and the floor. As in all of Demuth's *In Vaudeville* or *Acrobat* series, Demuth empathized with each and every performer. Even the chorus girls are depicted as deeply involved in their act.

1918. Watercolor on paper,
12⅞ × 7¹¹⁄₁₆ in. (32.7 × 19.5 cm).
The Philadelphia Museum of Art:
The A. E. Gallatin Collection.

Demuth —   " Flora "   " She had picked up small flat piece. "

Plate 19
FLORA AND THE GOVERNESS

In his illustrations, particularly those for *The Turn of the Screw* and *The Beast in the Jungle*, Charles Demuth realized his optimum as an artist, a draftsman, and an illustrator. This happy amalgam was undoubtedly achieved by the painter's empathy for Henry James and the tales he chose to illustrate.

Although the color of *Flora and the Governess* is much lighter and more springlike in its tones than those found in the other illustrations, it conveys a feeling of built-in terror. Flowers are scattered here and there, and the lake and the boat appear unmenacing, but Demuth has also filled *Flora and the Governess* with strange shapes and forms. The tree trunks behind the governess, and the macabre hanging legs and plant forms to Flora's right create an eerie air. The governess is openly surprised by what she sees on the other side of the water, while Flora appears to be disturbed by something she sees in the water. The demonic presence of Miss Jessel, the children's former governess, is fully felt. In both James's tale and in Demuth's painting there is an unseen horror that is perfectly expressed by the gestures of the governess and the waiting figure of the young girl.

This is a splendidly envisioned and masterful illustration. Demuth uses his technical abilities to their fullest here to create an increasing sense of foreboding and terror. The cool tones are alleviated only by the light pink color of Flora's dress. The gray black tones of the governess's hat and dress are echoed in the area of the hanging forms and seem to point the viewer's eye to the mystery. Every element in the painting—branches, flowers, lilypads, tree trunks, leaves—all serve to heighten the mood of the impending horror.

Illustration #3 for Henry James's
The Turn of the Screw.
1918. Watercolor and pencil on paper,
8 × 10⅜ in. (20.3 × 26.4 cm).
The Philadelphia Museum of Art.
Given by Frank and Alice Osborn.

Plate 20 (right)
DELPHINIUM

This floral work combines four sprays of delphiniums in the blue and purple tones together with their leaves and the pale red buds of another flower. Every spray of *Delphinium* moves upward to make an oval-shaped composition. The gray and yellow-gray washes of the background complete the outlines of the flowers. This background defines the forms of stems, blossoms, and leaves. Although most of the blossoms are painted and then blotted individually, occasionally one will appear to merge into the next flower.

In this watercolor it is apparent that Demuth's wash-and-blotter method, his knowledge of flora, and his own aesthetic development have all matured. There is absolutely no hesitancy in his brushwork or in his technique. *Delphinium* is another beautifully composed step in Demuth's growth toward artistic simplicity and perception.

1918. Watercolor on paper,
17¾ × 11½ in. (45.1 × 29.2 cm).
Courtesy of Kennedy Galleries, Inc., New York.

Plate 21 (far right)
FLOWERS

Although there are three different kinds of flowers in this watercolor, the primary subject is the four handsomely painted irises. To the upper right is a delicate sprig of flowers painted in the palest tones of pink, and at the lower right and in the center of the irises are two small pink flowers. A fragile beauty pervades the painting; the pencil underdrawing is sketched and the paint is lightly washed. Demuth's mastery of the blotter technique is apparent in the mottled mauves and muted gray greens of the irises.

All the colors in this floral partake of the shades and tones of the irises. The palest tones are mixed with the greens to create the olive color, which gives the entire watercolor a lovely uniformity of color values. There are little or no color differences in the various leaves and stems, and the flowers share a lavender-to-purple-to-rose mutuality. Demuth treats each flower as an entity which belongs to a lovely whole.

1919. Watercolor and pencil on paper,
17⅝ × 11⅝ in. (44.5 × 29.2 cm).
Private Collection, Courtesy: Andrew Crispo Gallery, New York.

Plate 22
MARCHER RECEIVES HIS REVELATION AT
MAY BARTRAM'S TOMB

Marcher Receives His Revelation at May Bartram's Tomb is the final illustration for *The Beast in the Jungle* by Henry James. Demuth clearly understood the essential differences between *The Turn of the Screw* and *The Beast in the Jungle*. In this work there is nothing unseen. Instead, Demuth depicted the remorse of a man who has left things unsaid and affection unexpressed. It is only after May Bartram has died that John Marcher is able to understand what he should have said to her. Since that is no longer possible, he feels a desperate desolation. At last the overcautious Marcher throws himself on Miss Bartram's grave, scattering his derby, his cane, and his gloves in his final realization.

With the exception of John Marcher's clothes, the color here is almost nonexistent. The pale-lemon ocher, the traces of pale-red ocher, and the soft Vandyke brown all reflect the colorlessness of John Marcher. Every tone is muted; Demuth uses his pencil to darken and negate any sense of color, as well as to indicate the grass, trees, and gravestones. A ring of winter tree trunks encircles the background of the painting and brings the viewer back to the despairing figure of Marcher and his scattered belongings.

Illustration #3 for Henry James's
The Beast in the Jungle.
1919. Watercolor and pencil on paper,
8 × 10 in. (20.3 × 25.4 cm).
The Philadelphia Museum of Art.
Given by Frank and Alice Osborn.

Plate 23 (right)
BOX OF TRICKS

In 1919 Charles Demuth started a new series of paintings in tempera, all of them larger than his previous watercolors. The titles of these 1919 works are Duchampian and notable for their double-entendre, such as *Box of Tricks, Backdrop for East Lynn, Rise of the Prism, In the Province, In the Key of Blue*, and *Gloucester* or *Mackerel 35¢ a Pound*. These semiabstract landscapes are original to Demuth and incorporate his own Cubist techniques in which he used prisms, facetings, spotlight effects—all those elements which add up to a "box of tricks."

A Gloucester steeple and meeting house make up the primary forms of the composition viewed from the ocean. Two ship masts rise out of the painting, one to the left and two to the right, the farthest of which frames the painting. The two reddish-toned roofs and the blue shape above them are the only areas of true color in the painting. All else is tan, gray beige, off-white, or a very dark brown. The diagonal lines of the sails attached to the three masts create the facetings and rays of this Cubist-inspired architectural landscape. *Box of Tricks* is aptly titled; the artist has devised a magical abstract landscape that teases and charms the viewer.

1919. Tempera on academy board,
19½ × 15¼ in. (49.5 × 38.7 cm).
The Philadelphia Museum of Art:
Purchased: The Edgar Viguers Seeler Fund.

Plate 24 (far right)
BUILDINGS

This superbly elegant tempera painting is closely aligned with the Demuth temperas and oils of the 1919–1920 period and to a 1931 work, *Chimney and Water Tower*. However, *Buildings* is simpler than any of these and has a much more vertical composition. It is only the seemingly arbitrary ray lines that counteract the strong verticality. Because the rays do not emerge from an understood source is also a new element in Demuth's design. The two watertowers are painted in deep tones of red turning to black, and the chimney, which almost splits the composition, is an ocherous green. The other colors range from blue to black grays and form the smoke swirls of the chimney to the right as well as that of the trio of chimneys below the left watertower.

The title of *Buildings* is a key to the date of this tempera. Its ironic, Duchampian description of water towers and belching chimneys implies that Demuth considered these to be the "buildings" of the future.

c. 1920. Tempera on academy board,
29¾ × 24 in. (75.6 × 61 cm).
Private collection, photograph courtesy
James Maroney, Inc.

Plate 25
TIGER LILIES

In this lovely composition of intertwining tiger lilies, Demuth made great strides in his use of the watercolor medium. He has used the negative spaces of the paper superbly; by leaving some of the flowers unpainted Demuth has made this painting sparkle. Looking back on such paintings as *Allover Pattern of Lilacs* or *Flower Piece*, both painted in 1915, it is apparent that the Cubist and Cézanne influences have added to the vigor and lucidity of *Tiger Lilies*.

Demuth's knowledge of flora and his ability to compose several plants or flowers for his own design are almost without equal. His colors scintillate here; his technical mastery is exceeded only by the beauty he has created.

The movement in *Tiger Lilies* is atypical in Demuth's florals. Instead of the flowers reaching upward, here some of the lilies and the buds are pendant. Almost magically, however, there is still a sense of vertical movement coming from the area of the main stem behind the flowers. Demuth plays with the color, the spotted design of the blossoms, and the soft olive greens of the leaves, creating a stunning pattern of lights and darks.

1920. Watercolor and pencil on paper,
8¼ × 12 (21.1 × 30.5 cm).
Private collection.
Courtesy of Sotheby Parke Bernet, New York.

Plate 26 (left)
RUE DU SINGE QUI PÊCHE

This fine tempera, named after the Parisian "Street of the Monkey Who Fishes," was painted during Demuth's last visit to Paris. The painting has an atmosphere of seclusion, depicting one of those many Parisian streets that suddenly turns into a cul-de-sac.

The colors in *Rue du Singe Qui Pêche* are mainly blue grays and grayed ochers. The only relief from the neutral color is provided by some muted reds and the off-white of two of the buildings. Despite this limited palette, the painting has a radiant quality that is caused partly by the shaft of sunlight dramatically striking the five vertical buildings and reflecting back on the foreground building.

Rue du Singe Qui Pêche is framed on both sides by buildings. The foreground contains the darkest tones, which are enlivened by the many signs and shutters. The one patch of white sky in the background is intersected by two red chimneys, an effect that enhances the intense feeling of enclosure. The structure of the painting is almost completely vertical, interrupted only by the horizontal bands of the sunlight, the signs, and two balconies. This could only be Paris—never Lancaster or Gloucester.

1921. Tempera on academy board,
21 × 16 in. (53.3 × 40.6 cm).
Private collection.

Plate 27 (above)
MODERN CONVENIENCES

This architectural oil dates from the year of Demuth's onset of diabetes. With the debility this disease often exerts, it may well have been that Demuth found tempera and oil "easier" than watercolor. The subject of *Modern Conveniences* is the rear entrance of a factory building—a mélange of staircases, ladders, and fire escapes, all painted in black. Demuth's title must once more be taken as a sardonic comment on the inelegance of iron railings, ladders, and steps, all of which must have been an added inconvenience to the lame artist.

At the right an arc quite arbitrarily intersects the pale brick building and continues up into the blue mauve sky. A ray of sunlight moves through the center of the painting, and another ray cuts across the sky.

The painting is framed by dark areas. Although the direction of the work is horizontal there are three main verticals on the left.

The colors in *Modern Conveniences* are restricted to shades of red in the large buildings. The other forms, other than the mauve blue sky, are painted in a variety of grays, from off-white to almost black. Even with this limited range, however, the painting conveys a vibrant, brilliant quality.

1921. Oil on canvas,
25¹³⁄₁₆ × 21⅛ in. (65.6 × 53.7 cm).
Columbus Museum of Art, Columbus, Ohio.
Gift of Ferdinand Howald.

Plate 28
FROM THE GARDEN OF THE CHÂTEAU

This painting was most probably started before De-muth's last trip to Paris. It represents the vista from the lovely garden of his home on King Street—a view of the newly founded laundry replete with telephone lines, wires, and pipelike chimneys, all new to Lancaster. The colors are similar to the yellows, orange-reds, and olive greens of the water-color *Sunflowers*. Texture plays an important part in this painting. In this oil painting, Demuth manages to achieve the blotter effect used in his water-colors, particularly in the brick building on the left.

Structurally, the work is typical of Demuth landscapes: the lower half provides the horizontal anchor, counterbalanced by the vertical thrusts of the brick building and the two dark chimneys. Unlike many of Demuth's hard-edged works, the ray lines here seem to derive from actual objects in the painting—the wires and electric glass posts.

From the Garden of the Château has the most checkered history of any of Demuth's works. Around 1930, Demuth gave it on consignment to the Downtown Gallery in New York, under the aegis of Edith Gregor Halpert. Mrs. Halpert was unable to find a buyer, and she placed it, also on consignment, at the Boyer Gallery in Philadelphia, along with several other of Demuth's works. Juliana Force of the Whitney Museum of American Art became interested in these works at the Boyer and purchased, among others, *From the Garden of the Château*. Demuth never was paid.

The Whitney Museum then sent the painting on a traveling exhibition to South America. During the exhibition's travels, a fire broke out and *From the Garden of the Château* was singed. After its return, the Whitney collected the amount it was insured for, and the painting became the property of the insurance company. The insurance company, having no use for "art," gave it away to a business associate, a Mr. William Bender, Jr. He insisted, however, on paying one-third of the painting's original valuation. *From the Garden of the Château* was quickly and easily restored, for the damage was quite slight; it remained the proud possession of Mr. and Mrs. Bender until their deaths.

1921. Oil on canvas,
25 × 20 in. (63.5 × 50.8 cm).
Hirschl & Adler Galleries, Inc., New York.

Fele - 1925
C Demuth
Lancaster, Pa.

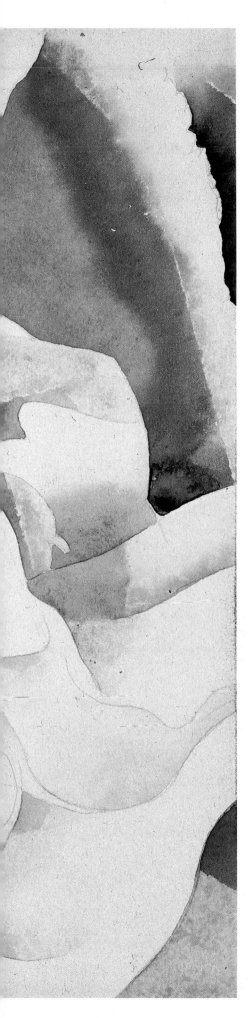

Plate 29 (above)
YELLOW CALLA LILY LEAVES

Because the motif is leaves and not flowers or fruit, this flawless watercolor is a rarity in Charles Demuth's work. Executed in myriad shades of green, from pale yellows to the richest emerald, its composition and technique can only be called masterful. With the greatest simplicity, using only the leaves of the calla lily as subject matter, the artist has created an exquisite economy of form. The assymmetry of the composition is controlled by the largest leaves—one leaning to center-right and the other leaning just slightly to the left. The leaves arranged in the foreground provide the central focus of the painting, from which the other leaves and stems move upward.

Demuth's draftmanship was truly at its finest here. Every twist and turn of each leaf is attended to with exquisite care. Each sensuous form is considered separately and yet is an essential element in the composition as a whole. It is, indeed, one of the finest examples of Demuth's extraordinary pencil line, sensitivity to the nuances of color, and command of the watercolor medium.

1922. Watercolor on paper,
19⅞ × 13⅞ in. (50.5 × 35.2 cm).
Yale University Art Gallery, New Haven, Connecticut.

Plate 30 (left)
APPLES AND GREEN GLASS

This extraordinary watercolor is one of two such still lifes Demuth painted in 1925. It is an example of Demuth's ability to combine the elements of Cubism with his own rather delicate but sensuous style. The apples and the glass in this still life are treated in a Cubist manner which is reminiscent of Cézanne. The faceting of forms and surfaces make a fascinating juxtaposition with the swirling curves and folds of the tablecloth and background drapery. The undulating shadows of the folds, the apples, and the green glass on the tablecloth add to this baroque effect. Demuth aptly balances these shadows with the shadow of the drapery background.

Apples and Green Glass is a tribute to Demuth's sense of composition and to his ability to incorporate major painting styles into his own work without losing his own individualistic style.

1925. Watercolor on paper,
11⅞ × 13¾ in. (30.1 × 34.9 cm).
Collection of the Art Institute of Chicago.

Plate 31 (left, top)
BOWL OF ORANGES

One of the most striking of Demuth's baroque still lifes, *Bowl of Oranges* is a tour de force in its dramatic combination of complementary hues. Executed with a boldness that presages the poster portraits and the later beach scenes, this still life seems to reflect Demuth's renewed sense of energy. It is as if Demuth in this colorful watercolor wanted to celebrate in paint the words he had written in his introduction to a Georgia O'Keeffe exhibition: "the ultimate shriek of orange calling upon the blues of heaven for relief or support."

There is an enormous diversity of color in the faceted oranges, the flower, and the three bananas. Here and there are shades of mauve or a spot of brilliant green giving definition to the drapery fold. The baroque style is apparent in the subject matter; the full sensuous curves of the oranges and bananas and the soft flowing form of the backdrop combine to make an extraordinarily rich painting. This lushness· is balanced by the rectilinear table, which provides a firm ground for the composition. *Bowl of Oranges* is certainly one of Demuth's most brilliant and complex still lifes.

1925. Watercolor on paper,
13½ × 19¾ in. (34 × 50 cm).
Columbus Museum of Art, Columbus, Ohio.
Gift of Ferdinand Howald.

Plate 32 (left, bottom)
EGGPLANT, CARROTS, AND TOMATOES

This still life demonstrates Demuth's move away from the baroque style of the earlier works in this genre to the far greater simplicity of the later still lifes. Similar to Demuth's other works with the eggplant theme, the sumptuous oval shape of the eggplant is contrasted with the rounder shapes of the tomatoes and apples and with the smaller, lengthier carrots. The artist has left much unsaid or understated here, and as became increasingly apparent in Demuth's later work, a great deal must be filled in by the viewer's imagination. The prismatic circular shadows shape the composition as much as the vegetables do.

Demuth uses color here in ingenious ways. The apples reflect and complement the colors of the carrots, the tomatoes, and the eggplant. The cool tones of the shadows are used to relieve the warmer, more intense colors of the vegetables. These colors, which range from grayed mauves to deep blue greens, impart complexity to an essentially simple composition.

There is nothing extraneous in *Eggplant, Carrots, and Tomatoes.* Each color, form, and shadow is vital to the composition. It is in works such as this that Charles Demuth demonstrates his superb control of his watercolor brush and technique.

c. 1927. Watercolor on paper,
14 × 19 in. (35.6 × 48.2 cm).
Norton Gallery and School of Art,
West Palm Beach, Florida.

Plate 33 (right)
MY EGYPT

My Egypt is one of the two most famous and most reproduced oil paintings by Charles Demuth. The meaning of *My Egypt*'s title can be debated, although the subject matter is the Eshleman Company's grain silos in Lancaster, Pennsylvania. The artist may have intended to point out the similarity between these American silos and the granary that Egypt once was for the whole world. It may also mean, more succinctly, that these silos are the American "pyramids." *My Egypt* is the only oil that Demuth painted in 1927 and it is also one of his last architectural landscapes.

Demuth's intersecting ray lines appear in *My Egypt* to be coming from the sky. It is possible that the rays refer to sunlight, but as they emanate from at least two different directions, they probably reflect the artist's concept of light rather than reality. *My Egypt* has a solidity to it that is quite unlike Demuth's more delicate florals and illustrations. This strength is very much related to the title and to all its cryptic meanings.

Despite *My Egypt*'s faceting of light and intersecting diagonals suggesting shafts of light and shadow, Charles Demuth rarely strayed from reality; instead, he used the everyday environment for his own aesthetic purposes.

1927. Oil on composition board,
35¾ × 30 in. (90.8 × 76.2 cm).
Collection of Whitney Museum of American Art,
New York.

Plate 34 (above)
LOVE, LOVE, LOVE
(HOMAGE TO GERTRUDE STEIN)

From 1924 to 1928 Charles Demuth worked on several symbolic poster portraits of his friends and of those he intensely admired. During his last two visits to Paris he had met Gertrude and Leo Stein, and they formed a mutual admiration for one another.

Love, Love, Love, much like the other poster portraits, is simply composed. Demuth incorporates lettering into the composition, as he had earlier in *Rue du Singe Qui Pêche*. Here it is used as a reference to Gertrude Stein's literary works and her love of repetition; the numbers "1 2 3" on the black background and the three partially shown "love"s on the red background refer to this. The mask, which brings the two sides of the painting together, symbolizes Gertrude Stein's theatrical works and her deep interest in the new psychology. However, it may also refer to Picasso's 1906 mask-like portrait of Gertrude Stein, which Demuth undoubtedly saw at the Stein-Toklas residence.

The absolute simplicity and perfection of composition in these poster portraits, and particularly in *Love, Love, Love (Homage to Gertrude Stein)*, are a marked advance in Demuth's aesthetic development.

1928. Oil on wood,
20 × 20¾ in. (51.8 × 52.7 cm).
Thyssen-Bornemisza Collection, Lugano, Switzerland.

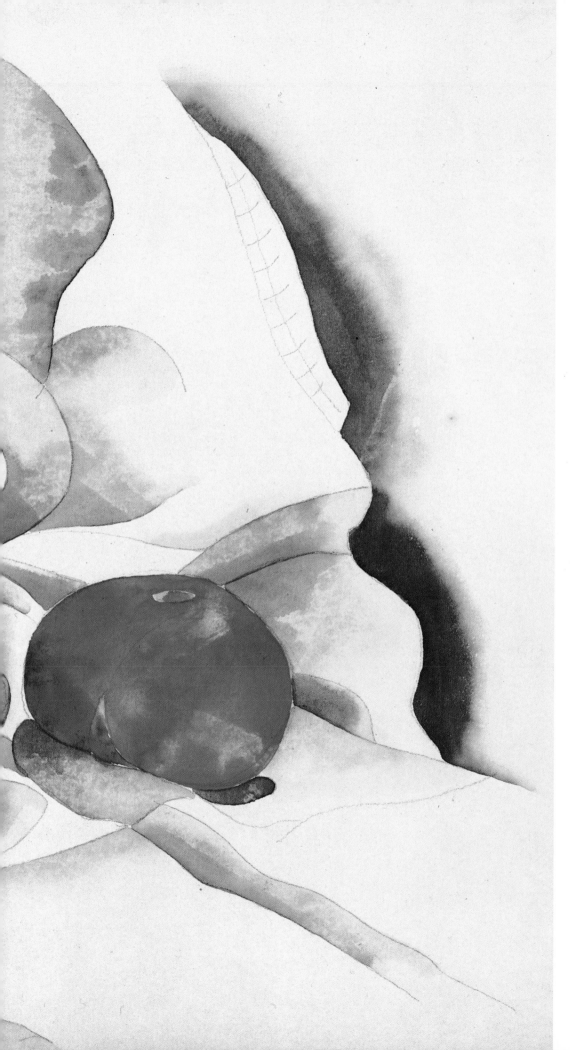

Plate 35
FRUIT AND FLOWER

Fruit and Flower is a perfectly balanced still life. Demuth's favorite flower, the zinnia, six plums, and three tomatoes form the focal point of the triangular composition. In this graceful watercolor Demuth uses the "unfinished" white areas of the tablecloth and the backdrop cloth to enhance the succulent contours of the fruit. The ripeness of the fruit is further expressed by the blotter method which captures perfectly their mottled, irregular forms.

By 1928 Demuth had been to Europe several times and had incorporated Cubism and the paintings of Cézanne into his work. Although this later still life has an essentially lyrical and gentle quality, which is characteristic of Demuth's style, the Cubist influence here is quite evident. The faceted forms of the plums and tomatoes are constructed by pigment applied in thin, almost transparent washes. This layering of color, rather than line, creates the interlocking geometric surfaces of the fruit.

Despite Demuth's obvious absorption of contemporary painting styles, his painting expresses a distinctive individuality. *Fruit and Flower* establishes Demuth's unique and important place in the still life genre.

c. 1928. Watercolor on paper,
12 × 18 in. (30.5 × 45.7 cm).
Private collection, photograph courtesy
James Maroney, Inc.

Plate 36

I SAW THE FIGURE 5 IN GOLD (HOMAGE TO WILLIAM CARLOS WILLIAMS)

This most well-known of Charles Demuth's works deserves its fame, as it is one of the most original and important paintings of American art in the first half of the twentieth century. It is also the best example of an artistically reciprocated relationship between a poet and an artist. Charles Demuth and William Carlos Williams began their friendship at a boarding house in Philadelphia in 1905. In 1928 Demuth painted *I Saw the Figure 5 in Gold* which was inspired by Williams's poem "The Great Figure."

> Among the rain
> and lights
> I saw the figure 5
> in gold
> on a red
> firetruck
> moving
> tense
> unheeded
> to gong clangs
> siren howls
> and wheels rumbling
> through the dark city.[†]

Williams was pleased with Demuth's portrait and wrote to tell his old friend that he thought it a "most distinguished American painting." The idea of a poster portrait as a symbolic homage to an artist that Demuth admired is original to him. Among other homages that he completed were those to Gertrude Stein, Eugene O'Neill, John Marin, Charles Duncan, Arthur Dove, Bert Savoy, and Georgia O'Keeffe. It is of interest that none of the poster portraits was sold during Demuth's lifetime.

In this homage to Williams, Demuth stresses the figure 5 itself, which is detached from the great fire truck that had carried it blaring down the dark city streets. The overlapping planes and the contours cutting cleanly into each other provide a unity of emotional expression that fits the urgency and tenseness of the poem.

That this is Demuth's tribute to William Carlos Williams is made even more evident by the red "BILL," the "CARLO" in gold lights, and the initials "W.C.W."

It is important to note that such contemporary American artists as Robert Indiana and Jasper Johns have acknowledged their debt to Demuth as an innovator whose paintings have inspired their work.

1928. Oil on academy board,
35½ × 30 in. (90.2 × 76.2 cm).
The Metropolitan Museum of Art,
The Alfred Stieglitz Collection, 1949.

[†]William Carlos Williams, "The Great Figure," *Collected Earlier Poems.* Copyright 1938 by New Directions Publishing Corporation. Reprinted by permission of New Directions.

Plate 37 (above)
ZINNIAS WITH SCARLET SAGE

Charles Demuth left all of his watercolors after his death to his longtime friend Robert Locher. After Locher inherited these paintings, it was his pleasant custom to give them to his nieces and nephews on their birthdays. *Zinnias with Scarlet Sage* is among those watercolors that was handed down through the Locher family. It has only been reproduced once before, even though it is one of the most beautiful of Demuth's later florals.

The zinnia flower became a favorite of Demuth's during the years 1928 through 1933. In this watercolor he combines the zinnia with sage and some wild flowers to make a superb bouquet.

Although the color range is limited to pinks, orange-reds, and olive-greens, there is not one zinnia flower that is like another in shape, direction, or color. This is also true of the sage and the other more delicate blooms. The inventiveness of flower arrangement, the multiplicity of shades of greens in the leaves and stems, and the delicate application of watercolor washes make *Zinnias and Scarlet Sage* one of the best examples of Charles Demuth's later florals.

1928. Watercolor with pencil on paper,
12 × 17 in. (30.5 × 43.2 cm).
Private collection.

Plate 38 (right)
RED AND YELLOW GLADIOLI

Demuth painted several watercolors with gladioli as a theme, but none has the finish or mastery of *Red and Yellow Gladioli*. The composition appears to be simply composed; the flowers, stems, and leaves form a floral triangle that is so deftly handled that its facility is not immediately apparent. The two branches of red gladioli enclose the yellow flowers, and the stems and leaves move subtly toward the right.

There is an inner richness in the flowers; each gladiola is treated as a graceful form unto itself and as part of the entire composition. The artist has considered every part of the design so finely that even the stamens and throats of the yellow gladiola are mirrored in the scarlet of the surrounding flowers. The rich greens of the stems and leaves provide the complement to the lively color of the flowers; and here and there Demuth has added a few fragile stalks of field wheat which lends a different form and texture to the painting.

1928. Watercolor on paper.
19¹³/₁₆ × 13¾ in. (50.3 × 34.9 cm).
Courtesy of Mr. and Mrs. Alan E. Schwartz.

Plate 39 (above)
GREEN PEARS

Years ago the critic Andrew C. Ritchie commented upon the debt that Demuth owed to the "true founder of Cubism, Cézanne." *Green Pears* is a handsome example of Cézanne's influence on Demuth. Cézanne's emphasis on the relationship of objects to each other and the building up of form with color rather than tonal contrasts is very much in evidence here.

The tangible substance of the fruit gives a definite compositional structure to this strong still life. Although the color range is quite limited, the clear yellow green of the seven pears is especially vibrant. The feeling here is one of intense respect for simple objects, even the humblest green pear.

In contrast to the early florals and the baroque styled *Bowl of Oranges* or *Apples and Green Glass*, this watercolor clearly illustrates a new development in Demuth's creative career. It has a still finer, more restrained, and subtle composition than any of his works heretofore.

1929. Watercolor on paper,
13½ × 19½ in. (35 × 50 cm).
Yale University Art Gallery, New Haven, Connecticut.
Gift of Philip L. Goodwin.

Plate 40 (right)
MAN AND WOMAN, PROVINCETOWN

This thoroughly charming genre work is a fitting climax to Demuth's short and astonishing artistic career. The heavily attired man and woman appear to be sightseers visiting the well-known resort town. Their posture indicates they have found something terribly interesting on the sand or out in the ocean.

In contrast to the more colorful beach scenes which were painted this same year, *Man and Woman, Provincetown* is subdued, even somber in its tones. Only the faces of the two people and the bow on the woman's hat reveal much color and then only the slightest tinges of red. The rest of the work is comprised of the muted browns and the gray blacks of the couple's overcoats. Their darkly colored bulk is balanced by the lightly painted and delicately drawn little dog pulling left on his leash. The end of the pier pole and the dune in the distance also help to pull the composition back into balance from the lean to the right.

1934. Watercolor and pencil on paper,
11 × 8½ in. (27.9 × 21.6 cm).
Private collection.

BIBLIOGRAPHY

MONOGRAPHS:

Farnham, Emily, *Charles Demuth: Behind a Laughing Mask*, University of Oklahoma Press, Norman, Okla., 1971

Gallatin, Alfred E., *Charles Demuth*, W. E. Rudge, New York, 1927.

Murrell, William, *Charles Demuth*, Whitney Museum of American Art, New York, 1931.

Ritchie, Andrew Carnduff, *Charles Demuth*, The Museum of Modern Art, New York, 1950.

DISSERTATIONS:

Eiseman, Alvord L., "A Study of the Development of an Artist: Charles Demuth," Ph.D. dissertation, New York University, 1976.

Farnham, Emily, "Charles Demuth, His Life, Psychology, and Works," 3 vols., Ph.D. dissertation, Ohio State University, 1959.

BOOKS:

Agee, William C., *The 1930's: Painting and Sculpture in America*, 1968, Whitney Museum of American Art, New York, 1968.

———, *Painting and Sculpture in America*, Whitney Museum of American Art, New York, 1968.

Arnason, H.H., *History of Modern Art: Painting, Sculpture, Architecture*, Harry N. Abrams, Inc., New York, 1968.

Arts Council of Great Britain in association with the Edinburgh Festival Society and the

Royal Scottish Academy, *The Modern Spirit: American Painting: 1908-1935*, Arts Council of Great Britain, London, 1977.

Barnes, Albert C., *The Art in Painting*, 3rd ed., Harcourt, Brace, & Co., New York, 1937.

Barr, Alfred, *Painting and Sculpture in the Museum of Modern Art*, The Museum of Modern Art, New York, 1977.

Barr, Alfred H., ed., *Masters of Modern Art*, The Museum of Modern Art, New York, 1954.

Baur, John I.H., *Revolution and Tradition in American Art*, Harvard University Press, Cambridge, 1951.

Baur, John I.H., ed., Lloyd Goodrich, Dorothy C. Miller, James T. Soby and Frederick S. Wight, *New Art in America, Fifty Painters of the 20th Century*, New York Graphic Society in cooperation with Frederick A. Praeger, Inc., Greenwich, Conn., 1957.

Bennett, Ian, *A History of American Painting*, Hamlyn Publ. Group, New York, 1973.

Blesh, Rudi, *Modern Art, U.S.A., Men, Rebellion, Conquest, 1900–1956*, Alfred A. Knopf, New York, 1956.

Born, Wolfgang, *American Landscape Painting*, Yale University Press, New Haven, 1948.

———, *Stilllife Painting in America*, Oxford University Press, New York, 1947.

Boswell, Peyton, Jr., *Modern American Painting*, Dodd, Mead & Co., 1940.

A. Praeger, New York, 1968.

Davidson, Abraham A., *The Story of American Painting*, Harry N. Abrams, Inc., New York, 1974.

Delaware Art Museum, *Avant-Garde Painting and Sculpture in America, 1910–25*, 1975, University of Delaware, Wilmington, Del., 1975.

Diamondstein, Barbaralee, ed., *The Art World*, Art News/Rizzoli, New York, 1977.

Eliot, Alexander, *300 Years of American Painting*, Time, Inc., New York, 1957.

Encyclopedia of World Art, vol. IV, McGraw-Hill Book Co., New York, 1961.

Faison, S. Lane, Jr., *A Guide to the Art Museums of New England*, Harcourt, Brace, & Co., New York, 1958.

Frank, Waldo, Lewis Mumford, Dorothy Norman, Paul Rosenfeld, and Harold Rugg, *America and Alfred Stieglitz, A Collective Portrait*, Doubleday, Doran & Co., Inc., New York, 1934.

Gallatin, Alfred E., *American Water-Colourists*, E.P. Dutton, New York, 1922.

Gardner, Albert Ten Eyck, *History of Water Color Painting in America*, Reinhold Publ. Corp., New York, 1966.

Garder, Helen, *Art Through the Ages*, rev. under ed. Sumner McK. Crosby, Harcourt, Brace & World, Inc., New York, 1959.

Garrett, Wendell D., Paul F. Norton, Alan Gowans, and Joseph T. Butler, *The Arts in America, The 19th Century*,

Brown, Jules D., and Barbara Rose, *American Painting*, Skira/Rizzoli, New York, 1977.

Brown, Milton W., *American Painting from the Armory Show to the Depression*, Princeton University Press, Princeton, 1955.

Bulliet, C. J., *Apples and Madonnas*, Covici, Fiede, Inc., New York, 1930.

Cahill, Holger, "American Art Today," in *America as Americans See It*, Fred J. Ringel, ed., The Literary Guild, New York, 1932.

Canaday, John, *Keys to Art*, Tudor Publishing Co., New York, 1962.

Cheney, Martha Chandler, *Modern Art in America*, Whittlesey House, Inc., New York, 1939.

Cheney, Sheldon, *A Primer of Modern Art*, Tudor Publishers, New York, 1947.

Christensen, Erwin C., *The History of Western Art*, A Mentor Book, New American Library, New York, 1959.

Clifford, Henry, introduction, *Arensberg Collection, 20th Century Section*, Philadelphia Museum of Art, Philadelphia, 1954.

Cone, Michele, *The Roots and Routes of Art in the 20th Century*, Horizon Press, New York, 1975.

Craven, Thomas, *Modern Art*, Simon and Schuster, New York, 1934.

Curry, Larry, foreword, *Eight American Masters of Watercolor*, Los Angeles County Museum of Art and Frederick

Scribner's Sons, Inc., New York, 1969.

Geldzahler, Henry, *American Painting in the 20th Century*, The Metropolitan Museum of Art, New York, 1965.

Gerdts, William H., and Russell Burke, *American Still Life Painting*, Paragee Publ., New York, 1971.

Goodrich, Lloyd, *Three Centuries of American Art*, Whitney Museum of American Art, New York, 1966.

Goodrich, Lloyd, and John Baur, *American Art of Our Century*, Frederick A. Praeger, New York, 1961.

Haftmann, Werner, *Painting in the 20th Century*, Lund Humphries, London, 1960.

Hamilton, George Heard, *19th and 20th Century Art*, Harry N. Abrams, Inc., New York, 1971.

Hayes, Bartlett H., Jr., *Drawings of the Masters: American Drawings*, Shorewood Publishers, Inc., New York, 1965.

Hoopes, Donelson S., *American Watercolor Painting*, Watson-Guptill Publ., New York, 1978.

Hunter, Sam, *American Art of the 20th Century*, Harry N. Abrams, Inc., New York, 1973.

———, *Modern American Painting and Sculpture*, Dell Publishing Co., New York, 1966.

Hunter, Sam, and John Jacobs, *Modern Art*, Harry N. Abrams, Inc., New York, 1976.

Jaffe, Hans L.C., *19th and 20th Century Paintings*, Dell

Publishing Co., New York, 1967.

Janis, Sidney, *Abstract and Surrealist Art in America*, Reynal & Hitchcock, New York, 1944.

Jewell, Edward Alden, *Modern Art, Americans*, Alfred A. Knopf, New York, 1930.

Johnson, Una E., *Drawings of the Masters: 20th Century Drawings, Part 1: 1900–1940*, Shorewood Publishers, Inc., New York, 1964.

Keaveney, S., *American Painting*, (*Gale Information Guide Library*), Gale Research Co., Detroit, Mich., 1974.

Kootz, Samuel M., *Modern American Painters*, Brewer and Warren, New York, 1930.

——, *New Frontiers in American Painting*, Hastings House, New York, 1934.

Larkin, Oliver W., *Art and Life in America*, Rinehart & Co., Inc., New York, 1957.

Lipman, Jean and Helen M. Franc, *Bright Stars: American Painting and Sculpture Since 1976*, E. P. Dutton, New York, 1976.

McCoubrey, John W., *American Art, 1700-1960, Sources and Documents*, Prentice Hall, Inc., New York, 1965.

McLanthan, Richard, *The American Tradition in the Arts*, Harcourt, Brace & World, New York, 1968.

Mather, Jr., Frank Jewett, Charles Rufus Morey, and William James Henderson, *The Pageant of America, The American Spirit in Art*, vol. 12, Yale University Press, New Haven, 1927.

Mellquist, Jerome, *The Emergence of American Art*, Charles Scribner's Sons, New York, 1942.

Naef, Weston, *The Collection of Alfred Stieglitz, Fifty Pioneers of Modern Photography*, The Metropolitan Museum of Art and Viking Press, New York, (published simultaneously in Canada by Penguin Bks., Ltd.), 1978.

Neuhaus, Eugen, *The History and Ideals of American Art*, Stanford University Press, Stanford, Ca., 1962.

Newmeyer, Sarah, *Enjoying Modern Art*, New American Library of World Literature, New York, 1955.

Norman Dorothy, *Alfred Stieglitz: An American Seer*, An Aperture Book, Random House, New York, 1973.

Novak, Barbara, *Painting of the Nineteenth Century*, Frederick A. Praeger, Inc., New York, 1969.

Pagano, Grace, *Contemporary American Painting*, (The Encyclopedia Britannica Collection), Duell, Sloan, & Pierce, New York, 1949.

Phillips, Duncan, *A Collection in the Making*, The Riverside Press, Cambridge, Mass., 1926.

Poore, Henry Rankin, *Modern Art: "Why, What and How?"*, G. P. Putnam's Sons, New York, 1931.

Price, Vincent, *Treasury of American Art*, Country Beautiful Corp., Waukesha, Wisc., 1972.

Raynal, Maurice, et al., *From Picasso to Surrealism*, Albert Skira, Geneva, 1950.

Read, Herbert, ed., *Encyclopedia of the Arts*, Meredith Press, New York, 1966.

Rose, Barbara, *American Art Since 1900, A Critical History*, Frederick A. Praeger, Inc., New York, 1967.

Rose, Barbara, *American Painting: Vol II, The Twentieth Century*, Rizzoli Intl., 1980.

Rosenberg, Harold, *The De-Definition of Art, Action Art to Pop to Earthworks*, Horizon Press, New York, 1972.

Rosenblum, Robert, *Cubism and Twentieth Century Art*, rev. ed., Harry N. Abrams, Inc., New York, 1976.

Seligmann, Herbert J., *Alfred Stieglitz Talking*, Yale University Library, New Haven, 1966.

Selz, Peter, *Seven Decades, 1895–1965: Crosscurrents in Modern Art*, H.K. Press, Washington, D.C., 1966.

Shapley, John, ed., "Charles Demuth—Painter," *Index of Twentieth Century Artists*, vol. 2, no. 10, College Art Association, New York, January, 1935.

Shoolman, Regina, and Charles E. Slatkin, *The Enjoyment of Art in America*, J. B. Lippincott Co., Phila., 1942.

Smithsonian Institution, *National Collection of Fine Arts*, Harry N. Abrams, Inc., New York, 1967.

Smithsonian Institution Press, *Pennsylvania Academy Moderns*, National Collection of Fine Arts, Washington, D.C., 1975.

Soby, James Thrall, *Contemporary Painters*, Museum of Modern Art, New York, 1948.

Stebbins, Theodore E., Jr., *American Master Drawings and Watercolors: A History of Works on Paper from Colonial Times to the Present*, Harper & Row, New York, 1976.

Sweeney, James Johnson, *Stuart Davis*, Museum of Modern Art, 1945.

Tashjian, Dickran, *William Carlos Williams and the American Scene, 1920–1940*, Whitney Museum of American Art, New York, and University of California Press, Berkeley and Los Angeles, 1978.

Taylor, Joshua, *America as Art*, Smithsonian Institution Press, National Collection of Fine Arts, Washington, D.C., 1976.

Time-Life Books, *American Painting 1900-70*, Time-Life Books, New York, 1970.

Tucker, Marcia, and Edgar P. Richardson, *American Painting in the Ferdinand Howald Collection*, Columbus Gallery of Fine Arts, Columbus, Ohio, 1969.

Wasserman, Emily, *The American Scene—Early Twentieth Century*, Lamplight Publishing Co., New York, 1975.

Wheeler, Monroe, *Modern Drawings*, Museum of Modern Art, New York, 1954.

——, *Modern Painters and Sculptors as Illustrators*, The Museum of Modern Art, New York, 1938.

Wight, Frederick S., *Milestones of American Painting in Our Century*, Chanticleer Press, New York, 1949.

Wilmerding, John, *American Art*, Penguin, New York, 1976.

Wright, W.H., *Modern Painting, Its Tendency and Meaning*, J. Lane Co., New York, 1915.

Young, Mahonri S., *Early American Moderns: Painters of the Stieglitz Group*, Watson-Guptill Publ., New York, 1974.

ARTICLES:

Allara, Pamela, "Charles Demuth: Always a Seeker," *Arts*, June 1976.

Brown, G., *Apollo*, December 1971.

——, *Art and Artists*, February 1971.

——, *Art in America*, November 1970.

——, "Kennedy Gallery, New York, Exhibit," *Arts*, Summer 1971.

Brown, Milton W., "Cubist-Realism," *Marsyas 1943–45*, (Institute of Fine Arts, New York University), 1946.

——, "57th Street in Review, Charles Demuth," *Art Digest*, March 1951.

Butler, J.T., "Charles Demuth," *Connoisseur*, August 1972.

Carmalt, S.P., "American Watercolors and Drawings," *Rhode Island School of Design Bulletin*, January 1972.

Champa, Kermit, *American Artist*, April 1975.

——, *Art in America*, May 1974.

——, *Art News*, May 1974.

————, *Art News*, Summer 1974.

————, "Charlie was like that," *Art Forum*, March 1974.

————, "Shapes of Industry: First Images in American Art, (Terry Dinenfass Gallery, N.Y.)," *Art News*, January 1976.

————, *Studio*, New York, April 1974.

————, "Washburn Gallery, New York, Exhibit," *Art News*, April 1975.

Coates, Robert, "The Art Galleries, Charlie Demuth," *The New Yorker*, January 1, 1938.

Davidson, Abraham A., *American Artist*, Summer 1969.

————, Art Forum, January 1969.

————, *Art in America*, May 1970.

————, *Art News*, Summer 1970.

————, *Arts*, December 1967.

————, *Arts*, March, 1968.

————, *Arts*, February 1970.

————, "Charles Demuth: His Stylistic Development," *Rhode Island School of Design Bulletin*, March 1968.

————, *Connoisseur*, December 1968.

————, "Cubism and the Early American Modernists," *Art Journal*, Winter 1966–67.

————, *Philadelphia Art Museum Bulletin*, January–June 1968.

————, *Philadelphia Art Museum Bulletin*, October 1967.

Davidson, M., "Demuth," *Art News*, December 18, 1937.

Demuth, Charles, "Across a Greco," *Creative Art*, September 1929.

Doty, R., *Art in America*, November 1973.

————, *Art News*, September 1973.

————, "Articulation of American Abstraction," *Arts*, November 1973.

————, *Art Quarterly*, Spring-Summer 1973.

————, *Burlington Magazine*, August 1973.

————, *Country Life*, July 5, 1973.

Eiseman, Alvord L., *Art in America*, November 1972.

————, *Art Journal*, Fall 1972.

————, *Art News*, November 1972.

————, *Art Quarterly*, Summer 1972.

————, *Art Quarterly*, Autumn 1972.

————, *Art Quarterly*, Winter 1972.

————, *Arts*, September 1972.

————, "Charles Demuth: Behind a Laughing Mask," (book review), *Art Journal*, Fall 1972.

————, "The Demuth Retrospective Exhibition," *Art Journal*, Spring 1972.

Faison, S. L., Jr., *American Artist*, October 1947.

————, *Art Digest*, March 1, 1951.

————, *Art Digest*, Summer 1952.

————, *The Art Institute of Chicago Bulletin*, November 1949.

————, *The Art Institute of Chicago Quarterly*, September 1951.

————, *Art News*, November 1947.

————, *Art News*, March 1948.

————, *Art News*, January 1949.

————, *Art News*, December 1951.

————, *Art News Annual*, September 1948.

————, *Carnegie Institute Magazine*, March 1952.

————, *Cleveland Art Museum Bulletin*, June 1930.

————, *Columbus Gallery of Fine Arts Bulletin*, March 1947.

————, "Exhibition at the Durlacher Gallery," *Art News*, March 1951.

————, "Exhibition of Water Color Drawings at the Durlacher Gallery," *Art Digest*, March 15, 1951.

————, "Exhibition of Watercolors, Temperas, and Oils at the Downtown Gallery," *Art News*, September 1950.

————, "Fact and Art in Charles Demuth's Architectural Pictures," *Magazine of Art*, April 1950.

————, "Fastidious Taste and Magical Craft: Exhibition at The Museum of Modern Art," *Art Digest*, March 15, 1950.

————, *Fogg Museum Notes*, November 1927.

————, *Magazine of Art*, March 1949.

————, *Magazine of Art*, November 1951.

————, *Metropolitan Museum of Bulletin*, February 1953.

————, *Philadelphia Museum of Art Bulletin*, May 1943.

————, *Studio*, July 1950.

————, *Werk*, April 1951.

Farnham, Emily, *Art Journal*, Winter 1965–66.

————, *Art Journal*, Fall 1966.

————, "Charles Demuth's Landscapes," *Art Journal*, Winter 1965–66.

————, *Philadelphia Art Museum Bulletin*, Summer 1966.

Field, Hamilton Easter, "Comment on the Arts," *Arts*, January 1921.

Geldzahler, Henry, *Arts*, May 1965.

————, "Numbers in Time: Two American Paintings," *Metropolitan Museum Bulletin*, April 1965.

————, "Reaction and Revolution 1900–1930," *Art in America*, August 1965.

————, *Studio*, August 1965.

Hagan, A.E., "Demuth Watercolors and Oils at the American Place," *Creative Art*, June 1931.

Hawcroft, F.W., "Acquisitions of Modern Art by Museums," *Burlington Magazine*, February 1971.

Judkins, Winthrop O., "Addition to the Wright Collection," *Springfield Museum Bulletin*, February 1949.

————, "Austellung, Museum of Modern Art," *Werk*, May 1950.

————, "Early 20th Century American Watercolors," *Minneapolis Art Institute Bulletin*, May 14, 1949.

————, "Toward a Reinterpretation of Cubism," *Art Bulletin*, December 1948.

Kalonyme, Louis, "The Art Makers," *Arts and Decoration*, December 1926.

Kenton, Edna, "Charles Demuth: Intimate Gallery," *Art News*, April 10, 1926.

————, "Henry James to the Ruminant Reader: The Turn of the Screw," *The Arts*, November 1924.

Lane, J.W., *American Artist*, February 1941.

————, *Art News*, May 1, 1937.

————, *Art News*, August, 1937.

————, *Art News*, March 26, 1938.

————, *Art News*, May 4, 1940.

————, *Art News*, February 15, 1942.

————, "Charles Demuth," *Parnassus*, March 1936.

————, "Exhibition, An American Place," *Art News*, January 7, 1939.

————, "Exhibition, Philadelphia Art Alliance," *Art News*, March 4, 1939.

————, *London Studio 10*, October 1935.

————, "Notes from New York: Memorial Exhibition at the Whitney," February 1938.

————, *Parnassus*, December 1937.

————, *Parnassus*, October 1939.

Lee, Sherman E., *Art News*, February 15, 1943.

———, *Art News*, January 1, 1946.

———, *Magazine of Art*, November 1946.

———, "Show in Washington," *Art News*, May 15, 1942.

———, *Studio*, November 1945.

McBride, Henry, "Charles Demuth," *Arts*, May 1958.

———, "Charles Demuth, Artist," *Magazine of Art*, January 1938.

———, "Demuth, Retrospective Exhibition at the Museum of Modern Art," *Art News*, March 1950.

———, "Exhibition, An American Place," *Art News*, April 18, 1931.

———, "Exhibition at the Downtown Gallery," *Art Digest*," July 1950.

———, "Modern Art," *The Dial*, December 1922.

———, "Nicholson, Stettheimer, Demuth," *Art News*, March 1951.

———, "Water Colors by Charles Demuth," *Creative Art*, September 1929.

———, "Whitney Holds Memorial to Charles Demuth," *Art Digest*, January 1, 1938.

Metken, G., *Arts*, February 1972.

———, "Berkeley University Art Museum; Austellung," *Kunstwerk*, January 1972.

———, "Lancaster Lens," *Apollo*, February 1972.

Norman, Dorothy, "Conversation with Marin," *Art News*, December 1953.

Phillips, Duncan, "Original American Painting of Today," *Formes*, January 1932.

Reich, S., *Antiques*, May 1973.

———, *Apollo*, July 1973.

———, "Reply with Rejoinder by Emily Farnham," *Art Bulletin*, June 1972 and March 1973.

Rose, Barbara, "The Politics of Art, Part II," *Art Forum*, January 1969.

Rosenfeld, Paul, "American Painting," *The Dial*, December 1921.

———, "Art: Charles Demuth," *The Nation*, October 7, 1931.

Schnakenberg, H.E., *Creative Art*, March 1929.

———, "Exhibition, An American Place," *Arts*, May 1931.

———, *Formes*, June 1930.

Seligman, H.J., "Letter to the Editor," *Art News*, April 17, 1926.

Sieberling, Dorothy, "Horizons of a Pioneer," *Life*, March 1, 1968.

Smith, Jacob Getlar, *Art in America*, Fall 1957.

———, *Art in America*, Fall 1958.

———, *Art in America*, Winter 1958–59.

———, *Art in America*, Fall 1960.

———, *Art in America*, Fall 1960.

———, *Art in America*, August 1963.

———, *Art Journal*, Spring 1961.

———, *Art News*, October 1957.

———, *Art News*, June 1959.

———, *Art News Annual*, 1954.

———, *Art News Annual*, 1955.

———, *Art Quarterly*, Summer 1958.

———, *Art Quarterly*, Summer 1961.

———, *Arts*, October 1958.

———, *Arts*, March 1961.

———, *Arts*, January 1964.

———, *Arts*, November 1964.

———, *Boston Museum Bulletin*, 1962.

———, "Demuth and Dove; Exhibition at the Downtown Gallery, *Art Digest*, April 15, 1954.

———, Detroit Art Institute Bulletin, 1953–54.

———, *Life*, March 28, 1955.

———, *Museum of Modern Art Bulletin*, Fall 1958.

———, "Parnassus, Coast to Coast," *Time*, June 11, 1956.

———, *Philadelphia Museum of Art Bulletin*, Spring 1963.

———, "Retrospective Show of Water Colors at the Downtown Gallery," *Art News*, April 1954.

———, *Studio*, February 1957.

———, "Watercolors and Gouaches Shown at the Downtown," *Art News*, May 1958.

———, "Watercolors and Posters at the Downtown," *Arts*, May 1958.

———, "Watercolors of Charles Demuth," *American Artist*, May 1955.

———, *Worcester Museum Bulletin*, May 1959.

———, *Yale University Art Gallery Bulletin*, April 1959.

Strand, Paul, "American Water Colors at the Brooklyn Museum," *The Arts*, December 1921.

Sweeney, James Johnson, "L'Art Contemporain Aux Etats Unis," *Cahiers d'Art*, Volume 13, 1938.

Van Vechten, Carl, "Charles Demuth and Florine Stettheimer in Pastiche et Pistaches," *The Reviewer*, February 1922.

Watson, Forbes, "At the Galleries," *Arts and Decoration*, January 1921.

Wellman, Rita, *American Modern Art*, January 1933.

———, *Amour Art*, October 1934.

———, *Art News*, December 29, 1934.

———, *Creative Art*, November 1931.

———, *Formes*, January 1932.

———, "Obituary," *Art Digest*, November 1, 1935.

———, "Obituary," *Art News*, November 2, 1935.

———, *Parnassus*, April 1933.

———, "Pen Portraits: Charles Demuth, Artist," *Creative Art*, December 1931.

Wright, Willard H., "At New York Galleries," *Fine Arts Journal*, December 1917.

———, "Modern Art: Four Exhibitions of the New Style of Painting," *International Studio*, January 1917.

———, "The New Painting and American Snobbery," *Arts and Decoration*, January 1917.

———, "Watercolor—A Weapon of Wit," *Current Opinion*, January 1919.

Young, Mahonri S., "Letter from Columbus, Ohio: Ferdinand Howald: Art of the Collector," *Apollo*, October 1969.

INDEX

Italicized numbers indicate illustrations.

Abstractionism, Demuth and, 13
Acrobats, 48, *49*
Aesthetics, Demuth's view of, 28–29
"*After all . . .*", 21, 22, 25, 26
After Paris, 10
After Sir Christopher Wren (or *New England*), 15, 25
Allover Pattern of Lilacs, 11, 36, *37*
An American Place Gallery, 22
"*. . . And the Home of the Brave!*", 21, 25, 26
Anderson, Sherwood, 11
Anderson Gallery, 18
Anschutz, Thomas, 10
Apples and Bananas, 18
Apples and Green Glass, 18, *68*, 69
Apples and Pears, 19
Architecture, 17
Architectural landscapes, 15, 16
Arensbergs, 12, 13
Arthur G. Dove, 18
Artistic strain in Demuth family, 10
L'Assomoir, Zola, illustrations for, 15, 41
At Marshall's, 38
Aucassin and Nicolette, 17, 25
Aviariste, 48

Backdrop of East Lynne, 25, 60
Bacon, Peggy, 26
Beach scenes, 12, 17, 22–23, 80
Beach Study, Provincetown, 23
The Beast in the Jungle, James, illustrations for, 15, 29, 41, 55, 58
Bender, William, Jr., 66
Berlin, Demuth in 10, 11
Bermuda, 25, 51
Bermuda: Demuth in, 13, 43; paintings of, 24, 51
"Between Four and Five", Demuth, 28
Der Blaue Reiter, 11
Blotter method of watercolor, 14, 43, 45, 47, 51, 75
Book illustrations, 21
Bouché, Louis, 13, 43
Bouquet of Jonquils, 21
Bowl of Oranges, 18, *70*, 71
Box of Tricks, 25, 60, *61*

Boyer Gallery, 66
Braque, Georges, influence of, 25
Breckenridge, Hugh, 10
Der Brücke, 11
Brushwork of watercolors, 33, 36, 56
Die Büchse der Pandora, Wedekind, illustrations for, 15, 41
Buckius, Kate, 10
Buildings, 25, 60, *61*
Buildings—Lancaster, 21
Buildings Abstraction—Lancaster, 21
Business, 17, 21, 25

Calla Lilies, 21, 43
Calla Lilies (*Homage to Bert Savoy*), 19
Carnegie Institute, Pittsburgh, exhibit at, 21
Carrots and Apples, 19
Cassandre, Alexandre, 25
Cezanne, Paul, influence of, 69, 75, 80
Characterization in Demuth's art, 29
Charles Duncan, 19
Chase, William Merritt, 10
Chavannes, Pierre Puvis de, 10
Cheese, Fruit and Vegetables, 19
Chimney and Water Tower, 21, 25, 60
Cineraria and Cyclamen, 43
The Circus, 44, 45
Circus scenes, 14, 45, 48
Circus Woman with Birds, 48
Coastal Scene or *Étretat*, 11, *32*, 33
Color, Demuth's use of, 18–19, 33, 34, 38, 41, 51, 71; in flower paintings, 16, 36, 43
Composition, Demuth's techniques of, 14, 15, 17, 19–20; architectural, 25; color used in, 41; spotlight device, 38, 48, 53; triangular, 43, 47
Cook, George Cram, 12
Cottage Window, 13, 14, 43
Crawford, Ralston, 25
Cubism: in Demuth's work, 51, 60, 69; influence of, 13, 24, 25, 75
Cubist-Realism of Demuth's work, 17, 19

Dadaism, influence of, 18, 25
Dana Watercolor medal, 19

Dancing Sailors, 14, 25, *46*, 47
Daniel, Charles, 15, 27
Daniel Gallery, 12, 15, 17, 41
Davis, Stuart, 12, 16, 25
Degas, Edgar, 14
Delphinium, 56, *57*
Demuth, Augusta Wills Buckius (mother of artist), 10, 22, 23, 27
Demuth, Charles Henry Buckius: aesthetic maturity of, 14; art of, 24, 30; "Between Four and Five", 28; death of, 23; disposition of works, 24; education of, 10; evolution of style, 25; exhibitions of works, 11, 12, 15, 17, 18, 19, 21, 22, 23; family of, 10; financial independence of, 11; homosexuality of, 11, 12, 23, 29; illness of, 15, 16–17, 19, 22, 65; influences on, 10, 11, 13, 16, 24, 25, 28, 43, 75, 80; lameness of, 10, 48; personality of, 24; physical appearance of, 23; productive periods, 13, 14, 15; self-portrait, frontispiece; style changes, 13–14, 16; travels of, 10–11, 16; as viewed by other artists, 26–27; wit of, 16, 19, 23, 24, 60; writings of, 26, 28–29
Demuth, Ferdinand Andrew (father of artist), 10, 11
Diabetes of Demuth, 17, 19, 22, 23, 65
"Distinguished Air", McAlmon, illustrations for, 21–22
Dove, Arthur, 15, 18; influence of, 13; poster portrait of, 18, 77
Downtown Gallery, 22, 66
Drexel Institute, 10, 20
Duchamp, Marcel, 13, 16; influence of, 18, 19, 25; *A Tribute to the Artist*, 26
Duncan, Charles, poster portrait of, 19, 77
Dunes, Prvincetown, 16, 25

Eakins, Thomas, 10
Eggplant, Carrots and Tomatoes, 19, *70*, 71
Eichholtz, Jacob, 10
Eight O'Clock—Evening, *46*, 47
Eight O'Clock—Morning, 47

Eight O'Clocks, 14
End of the Parade, Coatesville, Pa., 16
Erdgeist, Wedekind, illustrations for, 15, 41
Eshleman, Aaron, 10
Eshleman Company, 19, 72
Étretat: Demuth in, 11; paintings of, 33
Everts, Frank and Elsie, 22

"Farewell, Charles", Hartley, 16, 26–27
Farnham, Emily, 47
Fauvism, Demuth influenced by, 10, 11
Figure paintings, 11, 22–23, 27, 29–30
Fisk, Edward, 10
Flora and the Governess, 54, 55
Flour Mill or *Factory*, 17
Flower paintings, 11, 13, 15, 16, 18, 20–21; technique of, 17, 19, 36
Flower Piece, 12, 36, *37*
Flower Study: White Tulips, 17
Flowers, 56, *57*
Force, Juliana, 66
From the Garden of the Château, 66, *67*
Fruit and Flower, 74–75, *75*

Gallery 291, 17, 28
Georgia O'Keeffe, 18
German Expressionists, 11
Gertrude Stein, Picasso, 18
Glaspell, Susan, 12
Gleizes, Albert, 13, 24, 43
Gloucester or *Mackerel 35¢ a Pound*, 60
Golden Swan, 12, 13
Grapes and Turnips, 19
"The Great Figure", Williams, 20, 77
Green Pears, 21, 80, *80*
Greenwich Village, 12–13

Halpert, Edith Gregor, 22, 66
Hanging Plants, 43
Hartley, Marsden, 11, 13, 16, 18; "Farewell, Charles", 16, 26–27; influence of, 25, 43; poster portrait of, 25

Holliday, Polly and Louis, 13
Homages, *see* Poster portraits
Homosexual theme of paintings, 47
Homosexuality of Demuth, 11, 12, 23, 29
Hotel Brevoort, 12, 47; series of paintings, 14
Housetops, Seashore, 11, 34, 35

I Saw the Figure 5 in Gold (Homage to William Carlos Williams), 20, 21, 76, 77
The Iceman Cometh, O'Neill, 13
Illustrations, 15, 21, 29, 41, 55
Impressionists, Demuth and, 10
In the Key of Blue, 60
In the Province, 15, 60
In Vaudeville: Bird Woman, 48, 49
In Vaudeville: Dancer with Chorus, 52, 53
In Vaudeville: The Green Dancer, 38, 39
In Vaudeville series, 12, 14, 48
Incense of a New Church, 17, 25
Indiana, Robert, 16, 17
Intimate Gallery, 19, 21, 26

James, Henry, works illustrated by Demuth, 14: *The Beast in the Jungle*, 15, 29, 41, 58; *The Turn of the Screw*, 15, 29, 41, 55
John Marin, 19
Johns, Jasper, 16, 77

Kandinsky, Wassily, 11
Kiss-Me-Over-the-Fence, 21
Klee, Paul, 11
Kraushaar Gallery, 17

Lancaster, 17
Lancaster, Pennsylvania, 67, 72; Demuth in, 10, 11, 16, 22, 23; *My Egypt*, 19; theaters in, 14, 48, 53
Landscape, 14, 42, 43
Landscape paintings, 15, 67; architectural, 15, 16; of Bermuda, 24
Larsen, Darell, 22
Leonce Rosenberg Gallery, 16

Locher, Ann, 33
Locher, Robert, 11, 23, 33, 41, 78
Longhi on Broadway (Homage to Eugene O'Neill), 13, 20, 21
Love, Love, Love (Homage to Gertrude Stein), 18, 72, 72
Luhan, Mable Dodge, 12
Lulu, Wedekind, illustrations for, 41

McAlmon, Robert, "Distinguished Air", illustrations for, 21–22
McBride, Henry, 12, 27–28, 38, 41, 47
McCarter, Henry, 10
Machinery, 25
Man and Sailors, 22
Men and Woman, Provincetown, 23, 80, 81
Man with Book, 29
Marin, John, 15, 18, 24, 25; poster portrait of, 19, 77
Marinoff, Fania, 12
Marcher Receives His Revelation at May Bartram's Tomb, 58, 59
Marshall's, 29, 30, 38, 39
Marshall's (nightclub), 12, 29, 38
The Masque of the Red Death, Poe, illustrations for, 15, 41
Matisse, Henri, influence of, 13
Metzinger, Jean, influence of, 24
Modern Conveniences, 21, 25, 65, 65
Moore, Marianne, 10
Museum of Modern Art, 21, 22
My Egypt, 19–20, 21, 25, 26, 72, 73

Nana, Zola, illustrations for, 13, 14, 15, 27, 29, 41
Nana, Seated Left, and Satin at Laure's Restaurant, 40, 41
Negro Jazz Band, 38
Negro Singer, 38
New York City, 29–30; Demuth in, 12
Nightlife, scenes of, 12, 14, 29–30, 38
Nospmas M. Egiap Nospmas M., 17, 21, 25
Nude Descending a Staircase, Duchamp, 16

Oil Paintings, 13, 18, 21, 25, 65, 72

O'Keeffe, Georgia, 15, 18, 23, 24, 30; color used by, 18, 71; exhibition of, 26, 71; influence of, 13; poster portrait of, 18, 77
On Stage, 12, 29
On "That" Street, 22
O'Neill, Agnes Boulton, 12, 20
O'Neill, Eugene, 12–13, 20; poster portrait of, 20, 77
O'Neill, Shane, 12
Oranges and Artichokes, 19

Pandora's Box, Wedekind, illustrations for, 15, 41
Paquebot Paris, 17, 21, 25
Paris, Demuth in, 10, 11
Pascin, Jules, 12
Pencil lines, Demuth's use of, 34, 38, 41, 48, 58, 69
Pennsylvania Academy of Fine Arts, 10, 11, 19
Pennsylvania-Dutch influence, 16
Philadelphia, Demuth in, 12
Philadelphia Sesquicentennial Exposition, 19
Picabia, Francis, influence of, 25
Picasso, Pablo, influence of, 18, 25
Poe, Edgar Allan, *The Masque of the Red Death*, illustrations for, 15, 41
Pop art, Demuth's influence on, 16
"Pornographic" paintings, 17, 22
Portraits, *see* Poster portraits
Poster portraits, 13, 18, 19, 20, 25, 72, 77; Precisionism of, 21
Pound, Ezra, 10
Precisionism, 14, 17, 19, 21, 25–26; of poster portraits, 18
Prendergast, Maurice, 24
The Primose, 43
Provincetown, Massachusetts: Demuth in, 12, 16, 22; paintings of, 33, 34, 51
Provincetown Players, 12

Ray, Man, 10, 15
Red and Yellow Gladioli, 21, 79
Red Cabbages, Rhubarb, and Orange, 21
Red Chimneys, 15, 25, 50, 51

Red Poppies, 21
Red State of the Grey Church, 25
Red-Roofed Houses, 50, 51
Rise of the Prism, 60
Ritchie, Andrew C., 80
Rodin, Auguste, influence of, 11
Ronnebeck, Arnold, 11
Rue du Singe Qui Péche, 16, 64, 65

Sailors (and Girl), 22
Sailors with Douglas Sommerville, 22
Savoy, Bert, poster portrait of, 19, 77
Sexual element in Demuth's work, 29, 47
Sheeler, Charles, 25
Single Peonies, 21
A Sky After El Greco, 25
Smith College Museum of Art, 23
Spencer, Niles, 25
Spring, 17, 25
Spring and All, Williams, 26
Spring Clouds, 32, 33
Squashes and Red Apple, 21
Stairs, Provincetown, 16, 25
Stairway, Provincetown, 25
Stein, Gertrude, 11, 12, 51, 72; poster portrait of, 18, 77
Stein, Leo, 11, 72
Stettheimer, Florine, 38
Stettheimer group, 12
Stevens, Wallace, 25
Stieglitz, Alfred, 11, 15, 16, 17–18, 19, 28, 29
Still Life: Window with Plants, 43
Still Life with Spoon, 20
Still lifes, 14, 17, 18, 19, 21, 25, 71
Strand, Paul, 18
Strange Interlude, O'Neill, 13
Strolling, 29
Sunflowers, 66
Sunset, Marin, 15
Symbolic poster portraits, *see* Poster portraits

Tempera paintings, 13, 15, 20, 21, 25, 60, 65
Thomson, Virgil, 12
Tiger Lilies, 62, 63

Toklas, Alice, 11
Toulouse-Lautrec, Henri de, 14
The Tower (or *After Sir Christopher Wren*), 25
"Tree" studies, 14, 24
A Tribute to the Artist, Duchamp, 26
Tropical Plants, 42, 43
Tulips, 21

The Turn of the Screw, James, illustrations for, 15, 29, 41, 55
Two Avocados, O'Keeffe, 15

Van Vechten, Carl, 12, 13, 38
Vaudeville scenes, 14, 38, 48, 53
Venice, Italy, art exhibit in, 23

Waiting (or *Ventilators*), 21, 25
Watercolor techniques of Demuth, 11–12, 17, 19, 23, 34, 36, 38, 47, 53; blotter method, 14, 43, 45, 47, 51, 56, 75; wash-and-blotter method, 47, 56
Watercolors, 17, 21–22, 24–25; Bermuda series, 13, 24: "pornographic", 17, 22
Wedekind, Franz, 15, 41
Welcome to Our City, 17
Weyand, Richard C., 23–24
Whitney Museum of American Art, 22, 66; interior designs for, 11
Williams, William Carlos, 10, 20, 77; "The Great Figure," 20, 77; poster portrait of, 20; *Spring and All*, 26

Yellow Calla Lily Leaves, 17, 69, *69*

Ziegfeld, Florenz, 10
Zinnias with Scarlet Sage, 21, 78, *78*
Zola, Emile: *L'Assomoir*, illustrations for, 15, 41; *Nana*, illustrations for, 13, 14, 15, 27, 29, 41

Edited by Dorothy Spencer and Candace Raney
Designed by Bob Fillie
Graphic Production by Ellen Greene
Text set in 11-point Caledonia